"Women with controlling partners don't merely suffer blows to their self-esteem and confidence; they also gradually and insidiously lose their sense of who they are. Deeply validating and brimming with practical advice and wisdom, *Women with Controlling Partners* guides readers through the often subtle process of psychological abuse, helping them escape the confusion and shame that enshroud their experience by offering a detailed road map back to themselves—and their lives. Their journey is made all the more reassuring by the rich voices of women who've traveled the exact same path in Lambert's recovery groups and arrived at their final destination—freedom—feeling deeply empowered."

> **—Craig Malkin, PhD**, Harvard Medical School lecturer and author of the internationally acclaimed *Rethinking Narcissism*

"This book offers an important opportunity for the multitude of women who are in relationships that are controlling, but who do not resonate with the term 'intimate partner violence.' It presents straightforward information about the insidious consequences that can occur from being in a relationship with someone who is controlling, and the levels of harm that can occur over time that may not be obvious to the person herself. Through this book, the reader can receive support, clarity, and guidance from the thousands of women who Carol Lambert has listened to and has combined their collective wisdom and courage. Mental health clinicians can also benefit from this book in deepening their understanding of the complexities of these types of relationships and the importance of patience, collaboration with community resources, and the power of peer voices and support."

> **—Janet Yassen, LICSW**, Acute Crime Crisis Services Coordinator of the Victims of Violence Program at the Cambridge Health Alliance, Harvard Medical School faculty, and cofounder of the Boston Area Rape Crisis Center

"An eye-opening exploration of how women become trapped in dysfunctional relationships with their angry and controlling partners. This is a gripping narrative that can lead women on a life-changing journey from denial to knowledge, from understanding to recovery. As a survivor of domestic abuse, I found this book true to my experience. It validated my pain, exposed the tactics of my controlling partner, and showed the way toward reclaiming my self-respect and autonomy. I recommend this book to anyone who has experienced domestic abuse, and to all those who care for them."

—**Pamela**, survivor of domestic abuse

# Women
## with
# Controlling
# Partners

### Taking Back Your Life
### from a Manipulative
### or Abusive Partner

CAROL A. LAMBERT, MSW

New Harbinger Publications, Inc.

## Publisher's Note

Distributed in Canada by Raincoast Books

Copyright © 2016 by Carol A. Lambert
        New Harbinger Publications, Inc.
        5674 Shattuck Avenue
        Oakland, CA 94609
        www.newharbinger.com

Cover design by Amy Shoup

Acquired by Catharine Meyers

Edited by Jennifer Holder

All Rights Reserved

Library of Congress Cataloging-in-Publication Data on file

18    17    16

10   9   8   7   6   5   4   3   2   1          First Printing

*Instead of abandoning ourselves, we can learn to inhabit ourselves. The body is tremendously homesick for us, and it waits patiently for our return.*

—Denise Taylor

For my son and daughter.

# Contents

Introduction     1

1   Control in Relationships Causes Hidden Injuries     9

STAGE ONE: Become Aware—Recognize the Problem

2   Realize You Need Help     26

3   Take a Close Look at Your Partner     39

4   Overcoming Powerful External Influences     57

STAGE TWO: Deconstruct What Holds You Captive—Breaking Free

5   Dating: What You Didn't Know About His Behavior     74

6   From Dating to Commitment to Confinement     85

7   Resist Falling into the Cycle of Abuse     98

8   See How Life Becomes "All About Him"     114

9   Take Back Your Strengths     128

10   Threats and Physical and Sexual Violence     142

11   Recognize Your Injuries from Abuse     159

STAGE THREE: Reclaim Yourself—Only You Know
What's Best for You

12   Change Beliefs to Feel Stronger                      178

13   Empower Yourself—Take Back Your Life                 189

14   Moving Forward—What Do You Want?                     199

     Acknowledgments                                      215

     Resources                                            217

     References                                           223

# Introduction

Sitting in a recovery group for women with controlling partners, a thirty-three-year-old teacher named Maggie leans forward in her chair and says, "My closest friend told me she was worried about me and my relationship. I couldn't believe it. I know my husband can be outspoken, a bit self-righteous, and hard to argue with. But I never thought of him as controlling." Maggie purses her lips. "I'm not sure, but I am too nervous to tell him I'm attending this group. In fact, I asked Carol to leave a cryptic message regarding the time and place of the group sessions so he wouldn't find out. It then dawned on me that I'm intimidated by him. I'm here to figure out just what's happening in my relationship."

*Women with Controlling Partners* is for people like Maggie, perhaps like you, who need to get clear about their experience with an intimate partner, whether a boyfriend, girlfriend, or spouse. With the help of this book, readers can become informed about controlling relationships, learn of the impact on their own mental and physical health, and through a recovery process can become empowered to work toward a healthy relationship and recognize what's possible with their partner.

During two decades of facilitating recovery groups for women with controlling partners, my colleague Hadley Fisk, MSW and I have listened to more than a thousand women speak about being overpowered by a partner. While each woman experiences a unique ordeal, together they tell the same saga: a slow, insidious, and nearly invisible condition of coercion entraps a woman within her most intimate relationship. So well hidden, this entrapment can go undetected even by the woman herself. The deceptive twist is that it is the most unlikely person, the one from whom she expects caring and love, who creates conditions that slowly diminish her spirit and sense of self—who she is. Being unaware of what is happening, she naturally minimizes and denies the problems with her intimate partner. At the same time, the experience causes a loss of self-esteem and trust in her own perception—making it even more difficult to see the truth. Ultimately, she feels she is losing herself, or parts of herself. A controlling partner can make her feel crazy when she's not.

Many women encountering nonphysical types of abuse experience grave psychological and physical health symptoms. They do not attribute these symptoms to the abuse they endure, mainly because psychological abuse does not leave a visible bruise or scar. But it is deeply hurtful and can be identified when you know what to look for.

The fact that you've picked up this book means you already know a little about how it feels to be with a controlling partner. What you may not yet know about is the process by which you can recover. The word *recover* means "the return of something that has been lost" (Merriam-Webster 2016). This book will help you get yourself back and recapture the parts of yourself that you have lost along the way. Once you reach a place of understanding your experience and trusting your perception, you can feel empowered to act in your own best interest.

You will benefit from this book wherever your relationship falls on the spectrum of minor to moderate to severe levels of control. If you are unsure whether your partner controls you, this book can help you assess what's happening. If you have been with a controlling partner in the past and feel plagued by fears of being hurt again, *Women with Controlling Partners* can help you recover and know what behaviors to watch out for. Friends and family members who are concerned about someone with a controlling partner can gain knowledge and be in a better position to offer support. This book can also help mental health and medical professionals, clergy, and others who work with women at risk to provide informed care for those they serve.

## The Story of My Work

In 1992, when my colleague, Hadley Fisk, and I sought training in a battered women's shelter, mental health professionals were not paying attention to domestic violence. Yet, at that time, abuse by a husband was the leading cause of injury for women. That year, we conducted a review of clinical literature that became the backdrop for creating a unique group-based model for treating women in controlling relationships. We called the model Recovery Groups for Women with Controlling Partners. In the group sessions, we felt deeply privileged to witness the women's courage as they engaged the recovery work, and to witness, as they got stronger, their transformations. From this experience, our passion grew and compelled us to raise awareness about domestic violence and, in particular, psychological abuse.

We embarked on a journey of presenting and educating to community-based organizations and professionals in medicine, mental health, and law. We helped establish the first committee on domestic violence in our professional organization, National Association of Social Workers (NASW). I wrote an article for their newsletter titled "The Abuse of Women by Male Partners: Where Are All the Social Workers?" Over the years, as our recovery groups gained attention, the encouragement to put what we learned into a book increased. I wrote this book so that what we learned in our groups could become a tool or lifeline for individual women and readers everywhere.

Psychological abuse, like physical abuse, is used to gain power and control over an intimate partner. Unlike physical abuse, it is hard to see because it happens with words and demeanor, without physical contact—yet it is undeniable due to the psychological harm it causes. When we began our work, the prevalence and seriousness of psychological abuse—also known as emotional or mental abuse—was an enormous eye-opener for us. We witnessed that the controlling behaviors in an intimate relationship that constitute psychological abuse were more frequent than physical abuse. We came to know firsthand how anyone—irrespective of ethnicity, socioeconomic circumstances, religion, education, age, marital status, or the presence of children—could find herself with a controlling partner. We listened as women shared poignant descriptions of being in a "fog," explained their profound feelings of guilt and self-blame, and coined terms like "domestic hostage." Their feedback taught us what methods helped them take back control over their lives.

## Recovery Is Your Best Option for Feeling Better

By following the three stages of recovery outlined in this book, you can move through the same beneficial process as the thousand women who have participated in our groups throughout the years. In Stage One, you start from a place of not seeing, in Stage Two you move to seeing clearly enough to know how deeply you're trapped, and then in Stage Three you learn how to free yourself. You shift from minimizing and denying to recognizing how your partner's behavior falls within the realm of psychological abuse. By learning the coercive tactics—misuses of power and control—and their hidden injuries (Russell 1990; Dutton 1992), you can identify the tactics at play in your partner's behavior. When you do, their powerful effects start to lessen. You will see how these coercive tactics are hurtful and can render you confused, fearful, and unable to act in your own best interest. Understanding your own responses to the "hidden injuries" of psychological abuse is an important part of recovery. The more clarity you gain about yourself and your relationship, the more compelled you'll become to finish the recovery process that gets you back to your self—a stronger self.

### EXERCISE: Is Your Partner Controlling?

Here is a brief exercise with five questions that illustrate what psychological abuse can look like in action and that will help you recognize whether your partner's behavior is controlling. As you read through each question, recognize how often you are on the receiving end of this behavior from your partner. Is it "rarely or never," "sometimes," "often," or "very often"?

- Does your partner criticize you and put down what you say or do?

- Does your partner look at you in a way that nonverbally communicates a dislike or disgust for you?

- Does your partner blame you, even for things you couldn't possibly be responsible for?

- Does your partner refuse to take responsibility or blame for his own behavior?

- Does your partner behave in a way that intimidates you?

Take a moment to review your responses. If you responded with "often" or "very often" for all or any of the questions, there's a likelihood that your partner uses controlling behavior. Although this can feel disheartening, at the same time, recognize that knowing more can help you. If you responded "sometimes," it might be in your best interest to explore his behaviors further to see what they are and how they adversely affect you—even a little.

## EXERCISE: How Do Controlling Behaviors Affect You?

The following four questions will help you look at your reactions to your partner's behavior. With controlling behaviors that are hard to see, their impact on your feelings and reactions speak volumes about your partner's behavior. Again, for each question, recognize how often you feel and think this way. Is it "rarely or never," "sometimes," "often," or "very often"?

- Do you feel like you're in a fog, confused, and not functioning at your best?

- Do you feel responsible and blame yourself for the problems with your partner and relationship?

- Are you more tense or uneasy when your partner is around?

- Are you careful about what you say or do around your partner because of how he might react and what he might say?

Now, take a look at your responses. It's worthwhile to pay attention to the feelings that occur "often" or "very often." When you're with a controlling partner, these answers indicate that you're experiencing negative effects from your partner's behavior. I hope you can realize that it's in your best interest to take this seriously. If you feel something "sometimes" and you're unsure, but wish to get clear about your intimate relationship, then explore further. In either case, help is resting in your hands.

## Let Your Commitment Grow

As women work through the recovery process described in this book, they start reclaiming who they are and learn to trust their feelings and judgment again. These important benefits keep women engaged because the more they learn, the more interested and committed they become in changing their lives. If you stay with the process, I believe you will also have this experience.

In *Women with Controlling Partners*, I have included many stories from the women who have attended my groups. Although revealing details are changed to protect their privacy, these women strongly wish to share their experiences because they know you can learn and benefit from other women as they did. See yourself in their stories and use their experience to help you understand your situation. Use this experience to know you are not alone.

When your feelings and experiences are validated by what you read, pause a moment to fully take it in. I encourage you to do all the exercises. Keep a journal or notebook with you as you read and work through the chapters. Following through with recovery will benefit you in many ways, including self-awareness and personal strength—qualities necessary to successfully address the issues in your relationship.

## About This Book

Since women in heterosexual relationships experience abuse almost five times more often than men (US Department of Justice 2014), this book focuses on women. If you're in a gay relationship or are a man abused by a controlling woman, whether currently or in the past, this book is for you as well. Despite my focus on relationships with "her" as the targeted person and "him" as the controller, all abusive relationships are important and need to be taken seriously.

This book will move you through the same three stages that my recovery group participants have journeyed. In Stage One, "Become Aware—Recognize the Problem," you'll determine for sure whether your intimate partner is controlling. Gaining this awareness allows you to move out of denial or minimization, take your intimate partner's control seriously, and understand it as psychological abuse that's deeply hurtful. It's critical to obtain this awareness—the first step to improving your life—before you can understand the full depth of your experience with your partner or spouse.

Stage Two, "Deconstruct What Holds You Captive—Breaking Free" helps you examine your dating period, understand how control by a partner slowly gets started, know how the cycle of abuse creates false hope for change, and identify specific coercive tactics so you can see them in your partner's behaviors. Through this process, you recognize how your partner's behaviors disempower you through the hidden injuries that impact your mental and physical health. This is the core of recovery and during this stage you learn how psychological abuse results from coercive persuasion or brainwashing, which alter your thoughts and feelings and keep you trapped through a loss of trust in your own perception. By recognizing the negative beliefs about yourself that you developed as a result of your partner's abuse, you can begin to take back your strengths, feel as good about yourself as you did prior to meeting your partner or even better, and attend to the thoughts and feelings that you suppressed to minimize his abusive reactions.

You'll then move on to Stage Three, "Reclaim Yourself—Only You Know What's Best for You" when you can embrace your new level of awareness, grow trust for your own judgment, and feel empowered to decide what is in your best interest going forward. Ultimately, your new strength will help you play an important role in determining what you want and discover what's possible with your partner. The book concludes with a helpful resource section.

You'll benefit most by following the self-growth process guided in the progression of chapters as you read the book straight through, from beginning to end. I recommend that you take the time to do this for yourself—you're worth it. Now, I invite you to turn the page and take a step toward help and healing. I wish you well in your recovery.

# CHAPTER 1

# Control in Relationships Causes Hidden Injuries

To pick up this book is, in itself, an act of courage. I applaud you! With this book, you're doing something for yourself—a huge step for women with controlling partners. If you have a pretty strong sense that your partner is controlling, then I know you have some fear or trepidation about exploring this issue. If you are wondering whether this is your situation, then it's great that you are taking a step to explore further. In either case, you might worry about your partner finding out. If so, your worry is telling you something worth paying attention to about you and your partner. In the next chapter, as you begin the recovery process, I will share strategies for protecting yourself to reduce your worry while you work through the stages in this book.

Almost everyone starts this process with some level of denying or minimizing the problem. Your first challenge is to be open to the overview information in this chapter and start to look at how psychological abuse might be a part of your life now or in the past. Imagine this exploration as a gentle unfolding, a gradual opening to new insights about you, your partner, and your relationship.

## Abuse Is About Power and Control

At times I hear women say, "I wish he would hit me, because I know that's wrong and then I could do something about it." It's what Amy, a twenty-eight-year-old mother of a young child, hesitantly said. She quickly added, "I'm not sure if I should be here. I've never been hit.

He's a good father but just isn't nice to me." She lowered her head. "Perhaps I'm making too much of it." But, as Amy would eventually learn, a good father doesn't abuse the mother of his children.

Without pause, a woman who walked with a limp and wore a finger brace responded, "I've been beaten. I have a broken tooth and two fractured fingers—but the emotional abuse is far worse than this."

Whether psychological or physical, abuse is about one thing: control. Your intimate partner's mission is to take control in the relationship and gain power over you. Dominating you is his main interest and he doesn't need physical abuse to accomplish it.

Because physical acts of abuse and threats of physical violence in an intimate relationship are legally classified as criminal behavior and often labeled as "domestic violence" or "intimate partner violence," people often assume that if there is no physical violence or threat present, no abuse is taking place. As our society has become more educated and intolerant of physical violence, controlling men use psychological abuse and claim "I've never hit her" and insist "I'm not abusive."

Clearly, physical violence has our attention. However, it is not nearly the whole story of abuse.

## Psychological Abuse Harms with Hidden Injuries

If your partner strikes you, you can actually feel the abuse—the pain in your head or back or stomach tells you where you've been hurt. Psychological abuse harms with hidden injuries that are not readily seen or easily identified. These injuries are quite serious and can affect your life dramatically because they target a woman's thoughts, feelings, and how she sees things (Marshall 1996). They will affect her sense of self, her view of the relationship, and her connection with the world surrounding her. This is why psychological abuse impacts your psyche and sense of well-being to the same extent as physical abuse (Katz, Arias, and Beach 2000). Recent statistics reveal how frequently psychological abuse occurs and that we are paying attention to it more now than in the past.

Nearly half of all women in the U.S. (48.4 percent) have experienced at least one form of psychological aggression by an intimate partner during their lifetime. Women identified verbal aggression such as their partner's angry gestures that seemed dangerous, being degraded, insulted, or humiliated; or their partner's use of coercive control. (CDC 2010)

Since psychological abuse is hard to see, and nearly one out of two women experience it in some form, we all benefit from knowing what it looks like so we're prepared to recognize it and respond accordingly.

Betty was a thoughtful, tired-looking mother of three grown children who lived in a comfortable suburban community with her husband of thirty-four years. She had endured serious physical violence for years. Betty reported being slapped, punched, pushed, restrained, and thrown against a wall. But while the physical abuse had ended years ago, the psychological abuse had never receded. Even though she no longer felt constantly at risk of being physically assaulted, her husband's daily emotional assaults were wearing her down. Her husband no longer hit her but other than that, little had changed within the relationship. Betty hoped to learn how her marriage was making her feel "sick and tired."

## Psychological Abuse Hurts—Deeply

Psychological abuse, the aspect of domestic violence that's the most elusive, endangers women the most. Fortunately, since the late 1990s, research that reveals psychological abuse and its harmful effects has been increasing. We now know that women can experience ongoing trauma, which causes them to develop serious physical and mental health problems. One research study showed that their physical health problems resemble those of women who experience physical violence. And women facing psychological abuse are twice as likely to identify physical health issues as the women who are not abused (Coker et al. 2000). Some of the physical conditions women suffer include chronic pain, headaches, stomach ulcers, and urinary tract infections—all of which make living life feel even more uncomfortable.

An even bigger consequence is the traumatic impact psychological abuse has on mental health. Even subtle psychological abuse (undermining, discounting)—without overt psychological abuse (dominating, demeaning) or violence—can be traumatizing (McKibbin 1998). In fact, subtle psychological abuse correlates more with women's emotional states than acts of sexual and physical violence (Marshall 1999). Here are what the studies say:

- Psychologically abused women experience depression, anxiety, and low self-esteem (Baldry 2003).

- Psychologically abused women score lower on self-efficacy, which is how empowered a woman feels to make a difference, than women who are not abused (Ovara, McLeod, and Sharpe 1996).

- When psychological abuse is compared to physical violence and other types of abuse, psychological abuse shows up as the strongest predictor of post-traumatic stress disorder (Pico-Alfonso 2005).

- Psychological abuse by far makes people more fearful than any other type of abuse (Sackett and Saunders 2001).

- A controlling partner who ridicules personal traits, criticizes, controls activities, and ignores their partner causes a loss of self-esteem (Sackett and Saunders 2001).

These findings make a strong case that, when you live with a controlling partner, it's just not possible to feel well or to be at your best because you're at very high risk for a multitude of health issues, including post-traumatic stress disorder. Take a moment to pay attention to how you might be feeling given what you just learned. All the ways you can be impacted can be unsettling to hear.

There is one condition in particular I want to highlight. While your feelings of self-efficacy—feeling empowered to make a difference—may be low, that terrible feeling of powerlessness is something that you can change. The hurtful impact of psychological abuse makes it all the more important for you to educate yourself, since by becoming informed you can initiate a shift that can help you start to feel some control. This book can help you create this shift as you move to knowing and then feeling stronger and empowered. Then you will have the best chance to take back control of your life.

EXERCISE: How Do You Feel?

I want to ask some questions about how you feel. As you read through each question, recognize how often you feel this way. Is it "rarely or never," "sometimes," "often," or "very often"?

- Do you feel anxious?

- Do you feel fearful?

- Do you feel worse about yourself now than before the relationship started?

- Do you feel you cannot make a difference in your relationship?

If you answered "often" or "very often," your partner is likely to be controlling and his abuse has negatively affected your self-efficacy and your self-esteem. If you answered "sometimes" to most questions, you want to keep your mind open. Recognize that these conditions and your responses indicate there's a possibility your partner is controlling and you're experiencing the effects of that. You need to learn more to be sure.

## Your Low Self-Esteem is a Controlling Partner's Best Protection

It's important to know that your feelings of low self-esteem and poor self-worth, caused or exacerbated by your partner's behavior, work in his best interest. Research reveals that under these conditions women are more likely to attribute the abuse they receive to their own personal traits and are less apt to see it as a problem with the relationship or their partner (Katz, Arias, and Beach 2000). As you experience psychological abuse, you lose confidence and self-esteem—once this occurs, you are more likely to hold yourself responsible for the problems in the relationship including, at times, the abuse you endure. Your self-blame can become your controlling partner's smoke screen.

Blaming yourself for abuse is common for women with a controlling partner. Your issue is not that you are at fault, your issue is that you are taking on the blame erroneously. We are all responsible for our own choices, including what we say and do. Your partner's abuse is his responsibility and his alone. I know this will take time to believe. That's okay. In time, you'll get there.

Psychological abuse needs to be taken seriously by everyone in our society. It's destructive and devastating, in a number of ways, to the one targeted. Yet, as one woman pointed out, "Psychological abuse is not illegal." In the end, women need to take steps to protect themselves. Recovery makes you stronger by helping you get very clear who is responsible for what in your relationship. This is one of the most important tasks to accomplish in order to feel better.

## How Psychological Abuse Works

A controlling partner takes control by using psychological abuse tactics that coerce and persuade you to his way of thinking. In her well-received book *Brainwashing: The Science of Thought Control*, Kathleen Taylor (2004) explains that when an individual uses abusive tactics within a basic social structure, such as a couple or a family, it is possible to gain power over another human being. When this occurs, it is one of the most intense and damaging experiences for those involved. From the experiences of a thousand women, brainwashing is the best explanation I've come across for what takes place with a controlling partner.

Coercive persuasion, more commonly known as "brainwashing," describes what the controlling partner does to take over the life of someone he proclaims to love. Amnesty International's *Report on Torture* (1973) inadvertently made a significant contribution to the field of domestic violence by defining psychological torture (Russell 1990). The report shows that the sociologist Alfred Biderman and his colleagues invalidated the myth that American prisoners during the Korean War became submissive and collaborative with the enemy by mysterious and magical means. They identified that it was due to brainwashing. Biderman recognized that these results were achieved through manipulative techniques he called "DDD": Debilitation leads to Dependency and dependency leads to Dread. For example, debilitation can take place by depriving prisoners of food, sleep, or human contact that then increases their submissiveness. Brainwashing is used during incarceration with hostages and prisoners of war, and in concentration camps, cults, relationships, and families.

In the realm of domestic violence, investigators recognized that abusive partners use similar manipulative techniques or "coercive tactics" such as isolation, claiming superiority, and humiliation. Without bars or chains, coercive tactics used by intimate partners are just as effective to psychological entrapment in the home (Herman 1992; Walker 1980; Russell 1990). Biderman's coercive tactics in his "Chart of Coercion" show forms of brainwashing that are important to address in the healing of emotional abuse (NiCarthy 1984), and that will be central to your recovery process.

## Psychological Abuse and Western Culture

At some point in a group, someone will ask, "Are we all talking about the same man?" Your partner's coercive tactics are not unique to him but are, in fact, shared by many or most controlling men. History is full of male violence toward women and male domination of women. The belief systems embedded in history get passed on from generation to generation. Despite the many positive cultural and political developments for women since 1970, we still live in a patriarchy. Men are authorized and empowered more than women. At the same time, we need to keep in mind that not all men seek to control women. Also, those who do may have mental illness, depression, or traits or character disorders such as narcissistic, antisocial, sociopathic, obsessive compulsive, paranoid, or borderline personality.

If we look back at the historical laws beginning in the 1700s that supported domestic violence, we find that battering by men of their wives and children was legally sanctioned and was, in fact, a longtime practice in Western culture (Walker 1980; WomenSafe 2016). By 1994, we had progressed: all fifty states had a restraining or protective order by which individuals could be legally protected from their abusers. In 2005, the Violence Against Women Act was reauthorized, which improved the criminal justice response to violence against women. Between 1993 and 2010, fewer people experienced physical domestic violence and the rate of intimate partner violence declined 67 percent (White House 2016). For an eye-opening overview of the battered-woman movement that fought for these kinds of protections, see the timelines in the Resources section.

The decline of physical violence in intimate relationships has great significance for all—women, men, and children. However, in the realm of psychological abuse, many men still misuse power to control women without legal repercussions. When we as a society deny psychological abuse, we are, in essence, sanctioning the hurtful control over another in intimate relationships. Even without legal protection for women and others who are psychologically abused by an intimate partner, individuals will need to declare for themselves that this behavior is unacceptable and has no place in an environment where individuals and families look to feel safe and prosper.

## Traits of a Controlling Partner

While controlling men do not fit neatly into one profile, there are characteristics that are common among controlling partners. The variations indicate that certain traits are more prominent in some partners compared to others. Abusive men have also been categorized as distinct types (Bancroft 2002). Here I'll describe some traits of controlling partners that are frequently reported by women in my recovery groups.

- He needs to be in control in his intimate relationship and sees to it that he has power over you to ensure he stays in control.

- He believes he is in charge and expects you to be compliant. He will degrade and silence you to keep his dominance.

- He lies and bends right and wrong, distorting information to benefit him.

- He blames you and doesn't own up to what he's responsible for.

- He believes you have no right to speak up for yourself, express anger, or hold him responsible. When you do, he makes himself out to be the victim and accuses you of being abusive to him.

From his beliefs and attitudes, the controlling partner demonstrates his expectations for you. When they are not met, he can feel justified in behaving disrespectfully, hurtfully, and abusively (Bancroft 2002).

Ultimately, the controlling partner expects his girlfriend or spouse to be compliant. To ensure this, he makes the alternative so painful that you find it easier to give in to avoid the "hard time" you would otherwise endure. He uses many different kinds of tactics to do this, yet they are hard for you to pin down. A controlling partner constantly changes his behavior to keep you off balance, which fortifies his position of power and control.

Here is an example of an exchange between two people that illustrates what can take place with a controlling partner. Although Elly feels some fear, she has decided to speak up to her husband about a concern. You'll see that when he minimizes her concern, she repeats herself. Then, when he attacks, she switches to defending herself. Suddenly, her initial concern is nowhere to be seen because he has decided that he's the one being given a hard time. He gets the last word, which is a blaming accusation. In the following dialogue, my observations are in parentheses. Here is how this goes.

*She says:*   You shouldn't criticize me in front of the kids.

*He says:*   I didn't like what you were doing.

*She says:*   Couldn't you have waited until later to talk about it, when we were alone? (She restates her original concern.)

*He says:*     You're always giving me a hard time. (He doesn't like her speaking up about his behavior so he labels it as "giving him a hard time.")

*She says:*    No, I don't. I'm just trying to talk to you. (She clarifies her intention.)

*He says:*     Just yesterday you were nagging me about helping with the laundry. (He devalues her asking for help by labeling it "nagging.")

*She says:*    I couldn't get it all done. I needed help. (By defending herself over the laundry, she joins his move away from her original concern).

*He says:*     You're always bitching at me. I'm tired of it. If you planned better you'd get things done. (He devalues her behavior, blames her, and sees himself as the victim.)

With a controlling partner, it's common to experience trepidation when you decide to speak up about a matter important to you. You start out articulating your idea or purpose, but before too long, you feel unsure. Like Elly, even though you did not agree with him, you can lose focus or your belief in your original thought. You might shift to defending yourself. By the end, you're vulnerable to feeling you are at fault for what he claims you did. If asked later how this happened, you might be too confused to explain. If this describes your experience with your partner, it is likely he's coercing or manipulating you when you approach him so he can avoid addressing what's important to you.

The controlling partner makes use of whatever tactics serve his purpose. He discovers what works and determines his strategy by learning from his experience with you. He gathers information to exploit your vulnerabilities, using what you have shared about yourself, including your past, against you. He will say or do things that he knows will cause you to question yourself, to make you feel uncertain or uneasy. He might even use problems he has with substance abuse, childhood trauma, or other psychological issues as reasons or excuses for the way he treats you. In time, you're more likely to believe him and give in, or give up trying to explain yourself. Here are a few examples of how this can play out.

- If you are prone to feeling guilty, he'll find ways to make you feel guilty to sway you to his way of thinking.

- If he knows about your childhood history of being abused, he may justify his behavior by using it to point out that you cause people to abuse you.

- If you react angrily to his abuse (which is understandable), he focuses on your anger as the problem to deflect how he mistreats you. Women often feel conflicted about getting angry, so it's likely you end up feeling guilty about your anger—then he's off the hook.

Another way a partner can make you vulnerable is by intimidating and degrading you. With strong conviction, he declares over and over that "you're wrong" in your perceptions and that your thoughts or opinions mean "you're crazy." He mistreats you by humiliating you, calling you names, and putting you down. Eventually, you feel confused, self-doubting, and even believe that yes, you are wrong or even crazy. As a result of this coercive persuasion, you can become painfully vulnerable to internalizing your partners' harsh accusations that move you further from the truth about yourself and your relationship. When this occurs, a psychological entrapment is taking place. This is only part of the wounding taking place inside you.

## How You Become Trapped

A fifty-one-year-old woman shared this experience: "I was a severely psychologically battered woman, but until my husband was observed visiting me in a psychiatric hospital, no one knew it. My husband was sophisticated and knew how to leave no signs. His abuse was so hidden even I didn't recognize it. I thought there was something wrong with me, probably in my brain, that I couldn't 'do life' as other women did. He thoroughly convinced me—and my family, friends, and doctors— that I was completely incompetent."

You find yourself tolerating mental stress throughout your relationship without fully realizing what it's doing, how it's debilitating you. With these debilitating injuries, you can be more vulnerable to your partner, have difficulty functioning, and find it harder to stand up for yourself. Most women with controlling partners report negative changes but may not attribute them to their relationship or their partner's behavior until they learn what coercive tactics look like and the hidden injuries they cause. All of this may make you feel "crazy" but you're not.

Does your partner's behavior make you feel badly? In strong and sound relationships, for the most part, both partners receive respect, feel comfortable, and trust that the other person has their best interest in mind. In controlling relationships, you can feel tense or anxious around your partner or find yourself dreading his reaction to finding something out. Do you find you're often saying to yourself that "I'm always wrong" or "I can't get it right, no matter what I do"? Your controlling partner creates an experience in your relationship that can cause major negative changes in you, including:

- If you were confident and self-assured before your relationship, you may find yourself self-doubting and insecure.

- If you felt grounded and trusted yourself, you are likely to become confused and indecisive.

- If you were happy and content, you're apt to feel emotionally exhausted and anxious.

- If you were competent and thought well of yourself, you may come to feel unsure and incapable.

- If you once knew what you believed, you're at risk of losing trust in your own judgment.

The losses are many and profound. These are just some of the hidden injuries to a partner's controlling tactics that will be addressed in later chapters. Given these profound changes, I hope for now you can appreciate how difficult it can be at the outset for you to know exactly what is going on in your relationship and trust your judgment about it.

# Minimizing and Denying Can Be Obstacles

Maybe you're still asking yourself whether this book is right for you. Or maybe you've read the stories in this chapter and thought that your partner is not as bad as other men. Women can minimize or deny the impact of controlling behavior, not only for themselves, but also the impact on their children. I have heard many statements like "They're always asleep when he yells at me." In the groups, it takes a while for women to understand and notice the different levels of minimizing and denying they have been living with and grown used to. Let's look at what I mean by minimizing and denying.

To "minimize" is to make something bad or not wanted out to be a very small thing (Merriam-Webster 2016), as not a big deal. One woman recited a barrage of disgusting names and painful, humiliating put-downs from her raging spouse and concluded, "He really didn't mean what he said." Another woman shared that her husband had never been physical with her but later added, "He only shoved me a little." In both examples, these women minimized their abuse.

To "deny" is to say something is not true or to refuse to admit or acknowledge something (Merriam-Webster 2016). As women begin to suspect or know that abuse is occurring, it's common for them to say, "It's not really happening," or to look for ways to keep it from being true in order to preserve the things they hoped for in their relationship: trust, love, and happiness. In my experience, women who question whether they belong in a recovery process later recognize that their denial kept them from seeing the abuse. Denial and minimizing develop as a result of many conditions, including:

- coercive persuasion, brainwashing, and wounding from your partner

- a culture that generally does not recognize psychological abuse

- as a coping mechanism to get along and survive

- holding onto the dream of a loving partner who may make a wonderful father.

Earlier I briefly shared how coercive persuasion works. Now, I want you to recognize that by its nature it promotes denial, which is a state of not-knowing. Coercive persuasion and brainwashing keep you from perceiving just what is taking place in your intimate relationship. It can keep you thinking your relationship is better than it is and your partner more caring than he is. This will become clear in later chapters.

In summary, denial and disbelief, which are normal responses to highly stressful experiences, can offer ways to get on with life and survive. Here are some common ways women with controlling partners use denial to remain unaware.

- Their fear of making changes and fear of talking about painful feelings keep them believing in the illusion that everything is okay or that it will get better.

- They silence themselves in order to prevent their partner's wrath and to keep some semblance of a close connection.

- It feels intolerable to look at the negative impact their partner's control has on children.

Although denial may seem helpful for adaptation, it distorts your perception of reality in a way that can keep you trapped and powerless. You have better options.

Like most women, you may not fully know if your partner controls you and a part of you may not want to know if he does. Holding on to your hope and dreams of how you'd like your partner, relationship, and family to be can keep you trapped in minimizing and denying how things really are. It may keep you from looking deeply at your experience. Many women later recognize that their initial state of not-knowing was more a state of not-wanting-to-know about the psychological abuse in their relationship. At the same time, it's evident that a part of them chose to seek help.

## You've Got This!

You know more now about controlling partners and psychological abuse than when you started this book. You know that just like physical abuse, psychological abuse is a way for a controlling partner to gain power and control over you. You know that he does this through coercion or controlling behavior that's intended to confuse and keep you "off balance" and unaware since psychological abuse is hard to identify. You've also had an opportunity to examine minimizing and denying, the two common defenses against psychological abuse, to help you determine if they are in the way of your recovery. By carefully examining your intimate relationship, you can recognize if your partner's behavior is coercive and how it influences and limits how you think, act, and perceive things.

Picking up *Women with Controlling Partners* says you're willing to explore your intimate relationship to see what, exactly, is going on. Stage One of your recovery, which you're about to enter, will help you do this. These are challenging issues to think about and respond to, but stay with this process and you will experience positive changes within yourself and eventually in your reactions to your partner. Know that without recovery, what you experienced and felt before you read the first word in this book would only continue and most likely get worse. Commend yourself for forging a new direction for yourself, your children if you have them, and your relationship.

# STAGE ONE

# Become Aware—
# Recognize the Problem

CHAPTER 2

# Realize You Need Help

You're valiant to address your partner's controlling behavior. I commend you for taking this step. I also want to acknowledge what you're not doing—you're not doing something, however tempting, just to get along with your controlling partner. You may have given up many things, including time with friends and personal interests, to meet his expectations and keep the peace. Now you're doing something for yourself, even though you don't yet know what the outcome will be. You may feel excited by your choice. And you may also feel uneasy. You may feel anxious or even scared. These are normal responses and we'll work through them. Keep in mind that by staying with the recovery process and changing the way you feel and think, you will eventually be able to orchestrate what you want for yourself in life.

During this stage, you will get very clear about which of your partner's behaviors are controlling you. This knowledge is critical in order to move from not-knowing or suspecting to taking his behavior seriously—in fact, it is the critical foundation you need to improve your life.

## Recognize Control

While women may find it hard to see control at work in their own relationships, they can, at times, see how other women's partners control them. This can be a first step. One woman in a recovery group shared that when she saw a friend's husband degrade her, she then recognized how her own husband does that to her. You may have someone in your life—a well-meaning friend or family member—who has observed something about your boyfriend or spouse and shared it. Perhaps you've been told "He can be a bully" or "He's a bit controlling" or "He doesn't always treat you well."

It may be that the messages you get from others are strikingly different from your experience in your relationship. Perhaps someone has said, "What a nice guy!" about your partner. Yet, you know his pleasant public demeanor disappears when you're alone with him.

Another way you might recognize control is by paying attention to your internal experience. You might feel unsettled in your body: a knot in the stomach or tightness in the chest. You may feel constricted and tense. To help you recognize the internal sense of what being controlled by a partner is like, in addition to simply thinking about it, I offer the following exercise.

Imagine you are tied with a three-foot string to another person called "the controller." The controller is in charge of the string; he is allowed to move freely. However, you have to follow his lead. If he walks to the left, you go left. If he chooses to stand in one place, you stay still until he moves again. You watch him so you're prepared for what he does next and you become preoccupied with him and his behavior. In doing so, you're naturally less aware of yourself. You find yourself watching for the tiniest shifts in his mood and behavior. Over time, you think less and less about your own needs, perhaps without realizing it. It's hard to be free, as the world you move around in gets ever smaller. At times, you catch yourself focusing on just getting through the day.

Take a moment to see if this feels familiar, like the experience you have with your partner.

With a controlling partner, you get to do what you want without trepidation when he doesn't strongly object and react negatively. He can do whatever he wants, but he gets angry if you try to assert yourself. He can limit your access to money, ignore your opinions, and prevent you from pursuing your own interests. When one group of women realized this was how they were living, one insightful member blurted out, "We're domestic hostages."

# The Turning Point

Realizing you're hostage to a controlling partner can be a turning point in your life—the moment you decide you need help and that things need to change. You may have reached it already. This new direction can feel like taking back some control for yourself.

When I convene a recovery group, I begin by asking each woman how she came to be there. As the others listen to the storyteller, I can see their thoughtful expressions, their reassuring nods, and, at times, their tears. During the twenty-plus years I've been listening to women's stories, I have come to see similarities that are striking and compelling—even though initial reasons for seeking help may appear quite different from the underlying issues. Before we attend to your story, let's look at how and why the following women sought help.

As you read through the stories of these six women, look for how your experience resonates with theirs, bearing in mind that each woman recognized the need for help in a different way.

## Lila

Lila, a graduate student in her mid-twenties, called the local hospital's help line to get assistance for her boyfriend because he was threatening to kill himself. While speaking with a counselor, not only did Lila obtain help for him but also learned through answering a set of questions that what he was doing was really emotional abuse. During their three-year relationship, her boyfriends' suicide threats were one way of powerfully coercing her. Lila believed that she held his life in her hands and felt terrified to say no to him.

Coercion is a powerful way to persuade you to give up what you want or need. To successfully coerce her, Lila's partner made her feel scared and tremendously guilty if she did not pay attention to him or give in to him when he was distressed. He knew she was caring and sensitive to his needs, so this tactic worked well. When coercion involves the threat of suicide, it's even harder to see it for what it is because the stakes are so high.

## Julie

Julie, a young mother of a toddler, was married to a man who accused her of being unfaithful. No matter how Julie tried to reassure her husband, he continued to torment her. He then escalated his psychological abuse by shoving and pinching her. When his behavior escalated to physical abuse, she sought help—although she could have used it long before. Julie became terrified and told a friend. Fortunately, her friend had seen a notice about the recovery group at her local library. In her recovery, Julie discovered that before the escalation to violence, her husband had been psychologically abusive for a long time.

## Lucille

A thoughtful pediatrician invited Lucille, the mother of his eight-year-old patient, to sit and chat privately after her son's annual physical. He inquired about life at home. Sensing his genuine interest, Lucille told him about her husband's recent, terrifyingly violent outburst over their finances. He had pushed her onto the floor and stuffed her mouth with dollar bills. Fortunately, their son hadn't been present. The doctor was familiar with domestic violence groups in the area and referred her for help.

## Selma

One woman in her late fifties, named Selma, was referred to my group after years of therapy. Although her abusive husband had been dead for nine years, her trauma had never gone away. Selma held the trauma of their abusive relationship in her body and continued to blame herself for the terrible abuse she endured during a marriage that lasted more than twenty years. It had included angry outbursts, degrading name-calling, and physical violence, and she had lived with strict rules that had serious abusive repercussions when broken. Since Selma felt deeply ashamed, she choose not to tell anyone, which kept her isolated.

In the recovery group, she finally talked about the terrible abuse she had endured and learned that her husband's abuse was not her fault but a choice he made, for which only he was responsible. At the tenth session, Selma rushed in smiling with a fancy new hat and announced, "I'm ready to get on with the rest of my life!"

If you, like Selma, struggle with the traumatic aftermath of an abusive relationship, your recovery will help you to stop blaming yourself, to heal, and to develop trust in your own judgment.

## Nicole

Nicole usually adores the way Eva, her seven-year-old daughter, is so inquisitive. But one night she was taken back by her daughter's questions. With her father away on business, Eva asked, "Why do we have to watch what Daddy wants on TV? I don't get to watch what I like." After a few moments, Eva added, "Why does Daddy always get his way?" Nicole was all too aware of her husband's intimidating gestures and unwavering insistence on having things his way. After Eva's comments, she realized she hadn't successfully safeguarded her daughter from experiencing her father's control and this provided the final incentive Nicole needed to finally do something about her marriage. Her sister had successfully completed a recovery group and for months had been encouraging Nicole to join one. Nicole felt strongly that she couldn't ignore her husband's behavior anymore.

## Peggy

At forty-one, Peggy was emotionally exhausted by her husband's anger and abuse. Peggy's husband was a lawyer and gave her menacing looks, put down her opinions, and used the silent treatment—sometimes withdrawing for weeks. Finally, after a big blow up, Peggy became determined to get help and her husband agreed to couples therapy. After three years of counseling, Peggy felt disappointed and frustrated because neither her husband nor the therapist took his intimidating behaviors seriously. Peggy announced she would get help for herself and joined a recovery group. When she completed the Controlling Behavior Checklist and saw her husband's behaviors for what they were—psychological abuse—she felt understood for the very first time. From there, she worked to find out exactly what was wrong and took steps to address it with him. His strong desire to remain married and living with his children provided the incentive for him to begin his own treatment specifically for controlling partners.

## Starting with Caution

Although inspired to seek help differently—by a pediatrician, a therapist, a hospital's help line, a friend, and a child—all the women you've read about shared deep-seated fear. Their partner's reaction if he found out that they were exploring whether their relationship was controlling scared them the most. Whether they told their partner or he learned through other means, they learned he would perceive it as a threat to his control. These feelings are important to pay attention to because they are evidence of the very control you are committed to examining more closely.

For your own safety, proceed with caution and careful planning. At the first session of a recovery group, I ask women to provide information that I need to know to protect their safety—for example, if they prefer not to be called at home and what message I should leave if I am unable to reach them. Knowing these details, I can encourage and support them to be careful. You'll want to figure out these details as well.

EXERCISE: Is It Safe to Share This Book?

Use the following scale to rate how you feel about five statements.

1—Strongly disagree

2—Somewhat disagree

3—Feel neutral

4—Somewhat agree

5—Strongly agree

Record your responses to these statements:

- I feel too inhibited to share ideas with him.

- I feel unsafe disagreeing with him.

- I am fearful of telling him something he may not like.

- I dread his reactions and withhold my thoughts and desires.

- When I do speak up, he verbally attacks me, insults me, or makes devaluing comments.

Add your points. If your score tells you that it's mostly not safe to speak up to your partner, take this seriously—don't reveal that you're reading this book.

If you scored less than 10, you don't seem to have a problem when speaking up to your partner.

If you scored between 10 and 15, you might have times when you feel uncomfortable speaking up to your partner.

If you scored between 15 and 20, you have concerns and most likely hold back.

If you scored between 20 and 25, you definitely find it unsafe to speak up and might avoid speaking up altogether.

Many women who come to recovery feel fearful and avoid their partner's abusive interactions in any way they can. You may have these feelings too. You try to stay a step ahead of your partner by anticipating his next move. You forfeit your own needs and preferences to make decisions that try to keep some semblance of harmony. Your partner's behavior, the very reason you need to do this work, can also prevent you from getting help or following through.

You may not feel safe enough to choose what's best for you. If this is true for you, I encourage you to pay attention to what you feel; your partner is revealing the extent of his controlling nature to you. To give yourself a chance at recovery, take your nervousness seriously and make a plan that allows you to succeed.

# The Importance of Secrecy

Lindsey always looked forward to coming to the group because it was "three hours out from under his rule." Although she did not like lying, she told her husband she was attending a work-related computer course. For Lindsey, a successfully employed computer scientist, the end of a normal day included getting out of work and dashing to her car to drive directly home since her husband had clocked her travel time at twenty-three minutes. A few weeks earlier, when she arrived home late due to traffic, he appeared at the door with a menacing look and screamed insults about her stupidity. Right then, Lindsey said to herself, "That's it—there's no way can I keep living like this."

Keeping your work with this book a secret like Lindsey did may be important for your recovery—even if it makes you feel uncomfortable. As conscious adults, we all strive to be honest in our dealings with others, so it probably makes you feel uneasy and guilty keeping secrets from, or lying to, someone you are intimate with. Yet when dealing with your partner, you may have to keep secrets to get even the simplest things you need or want. As you work through this book, bear in mind that you can choose to keep your recovery a secret, even just for now. Take care of you—protect yourself first.

As you move through recovery, you will need to decide whether or not to tell your partner that you're working with this book. This is often the first decision for women entering recovery and many women wisely choose not to tell. They know their need for secrecy began long before and you likely know this, too. Intuitively, you understand the important role that secrecy will play in your chances to follow through, to keep with your commitment, and stay safe.

Unfortunately, some women who participate in the groups never complete their recovery after they tell their partners about it. Some women tell their partners because they feel a moral obligation or an internal pressure to state where they are going. Or they need help with childcare. Initially, their partners may agree, but after a few sessions they become less receptive, start devaluing the recovery group, and ridicule the women for going to sessions. This is when women regret informing their partners. These women get worn down by the harassment, eventually give in, and give up their recovery.

Controlling partners are hypersensitive to threats to their control. For you to take steps to examine your relationship—whether it's through therapy, a group, or this book—hits at the heart of their control. Devaluing and harassing comments women have reported include the accusation that "the group is full of angry women who just hate men." Actually, this could not be further from the truth, but a controlling partner is closed to your efforts to convince otherwise and hard to reason with.

Inviting your partner into this process at the outset may not be in your best interest. You don't want to let anyone interfere with your recovery or give your partner any chance to sabotage it. Right now, you have a chance to launch your healing in ways that help you get stronger, because this book is an item you can easily keep to yourself.

## What It Takes to Succeed

In order to maintain their secrecy, women with controlling partners who decide to recover face a variety of challenges. You'll face them, too. In this section, I offer you two lists: one that consists of challenges you may face and another that offers resourceful strategies you can use to succeed in recovery. I hope they'll inspire you and help you realize more fully just how cautious you may need to be.

### Challenges

- Going somewhere that your partner would disapprove of or just taking time away from him.

- Your partner's need to know what you do most of the time, including who you see and talk to.

- Your partner checking up on you by doing things like going through your things, reading your email, looking at your Internet browsing history, and checking your cell phone for texts and phone numbers.

- Your partner overseeing how you spend money and questioning payments for anything you purchase for yourself or that appears out of the ordinary.

## Successful Strategies

Here are some ways to protect yourself. As you read through them, consider other ways to protect yourself, in general.

- Ensure a safe environment for recovery by keeping your resources and confidants confidential.

- Create a reason to go somewhere that you believe your partner will accept.

- Make sure "revealing" items, such as reading materials or notebooks, are hidden away in places where your partner won't look. This is especially important if he rummages through your purse, briefcase, or anything else that holds your stuff.

- Establish a private post office box to receive mail you do not want your partner to see.

- Set up a concealed place to store important information or documents such as a car trunk, a locked glove compartment, an office away from home, or a neighbor's or friend's house.

- Plan ahead and use money that won't be noticed, like grocery money, to pay cash for therapy, a group, or other resources.

# Create Your Own Plan for Success

If you are afraid your partner will get angry, lash out, intimidate, or pressure you, take steps to take care of yourself. Feeling as safe as possible is the priority and a necessary part of your recovery. Careful planning will help you succeed, just as it has helped the majority of women in the recovery groups. I hope you're keeping this book in a place that only you can access. Only you know how careful you need to be and how to protect yourself. If your partner has ever interrupted your plans or activities and prevented you from doing something altogether, you know what doesn't work. Like Lindsey, you may find that if you fabricate a story you think your partner will accept, you'll get a better result. I honor your courage for taking these steps to help yourself.

All women in recovery need a time and a place to do their recovery work. To successfully complete your recovery, you must figure out how you can create space in which you can reflect on your own, or with a trusted friend, and work through this book. Here are some suggestions.

- First and foremost, keep this book and the journal you'll use to complete the exercises well hidden.

- If it works for you, camouflage your book and hide it in plain sight. One woman kept her self-help books concealed in dust jackets from novels so she could read when her partner was around.

- To work through each chapter, come up with a reason to go off on your own to a library, coffee shop, or friend's house. If necessary, tell him you're going to a place he'll accept and then go somewhere to work on your recovery.

- Prioritize your recovery when you have time at work, between work and driving home, or at home when your partner is not present.

- It's fine if you are able to only get small amounts of time here and there. Eventually, you will complete your recovery.

I want to reiterate that a need to create secrecy about having this book and engaging recovery speaks volumes about the stressful situation that you live with, day to day. I hope you deeply understand how much effort these circumstances require, just to keep going with your life. Have faith and trust that you can do this for yourself.

## Look at Your Relationship Through Journaling

Journaling is a great way to focus and improve your awareness of your self and situation because it requires you to slow down and pay attention to your thoughts and feelings. The process of writing will help you think about what is taking place with your partner and, by recognizing how you feel, learn how you are impacted. I offer journaling exercises throughout this book to help your recovery work.

For each journaling exercise, have your journal handy and find a quiet, comfortable place to sit. To settle into the moment, close your eyes and focus on your breathing for a brief time. If you'd like, inhale slowly, pause, and exhale slowly. This can be a way to calm and center yourself. When you're ready, begin journaling.

## EXERCISE: Sharing Your Story

We begin with your story. Like the thousand women who've done this work before you, you have a story worthy of being recognized. Let yourself acknowledge that. Pay attention to yourself as you reveal your story and the details of your experience. Take them seriously because by becoming open to them, you move out of denying and minimizing, and begin to take back control of yourself.

As you document your story, know that you'll safely and successfully store your journal, which will free you up to write what you truly feel and believe. Here are some prompts to help you get started.

- Briefly describe your relationship and how it started.

- How do you feel about your partner and your relationship?

- Name some of the best parts and the worst parts of your relationship.

- Describe what it is about your partner and the relationship that made you decide to pick up this book.

- What impressions do you have, after reading the first couple of chapters, that make you believe you need to do recovery work?

When you're done, take a moment to read your story. Give yourself credit for the truths you've allowed yourself to see. As you learn more, this story will grow and deepen and you'll become even more aware of your experience with your partner.

## You've Got This!

You may be ready to acknowledge the need for help with a controlling partner or you may still have questions about your relationship. Either way, it's important to proceed with caution. As you work through chapter 3, Take a Close Look at Your Partner, you will become increasingly clear about your partner's behavior. As important is that you will come to understand that when your partner controls you, he is abusing you. His abuse harms you in many subtle, yet devastating, ways. Knowing about this harm will give you insight and the tools to do something about it.

## CHAPTER 3

# Take a Close Look at Your Partner

In this chapter, you're continuing to build your awareness. Earlier, you took in information about controlling partners and the need to proceed with caution. Now it's time to take an in-depth look at your partner's behavior. Let your work in this chapter signify for you a solid commitment to continue the process of becoming aware, by looking— and actually seeing—just what is taking place in your relationship. As you do so, be sure you commend yourself for this effort.

## Getting Clear About Your Partner's Controlling Behaviors

At her first recovery meeting, a twenty-six-year-old single woman named Jennifer said, "I'm embarrassed to say I don't know how I ended up in an abusive relationship and why I stayed." Your recovery depends on coming into your own awareness and understanding of your relationship. Be patient with yourself. Don't expect too much too quickly. Your recovery process helps you to become clearer, stronger, and better able to make decisions for yourself.

The power of psychological abuse can weaken when women "get clear" about their partner's controlling behaviors. The same can happen for you when two things occur: first, you identify exactly what your partner's controlling behaviors look and feel like because not knowing this allows them to entrap you and hold you captive; second, you learn to deconstruct the mindset you developed as a result of the coercive persuasion your partner has successfully used against you. These include the hurtful negative beliefs about yourself that your partner's controlling behaviors inflict that can cause you to feel powerless.

Once you achieve these things, you'll begin to see yourself differently and more positively. You will no longer be the person to blame or who deserves to be given a hard time. Instead, you'll become increasingly aware of his abuse. You're likely to experience painful and sad moments as you make meaning of your experience because the person you expected to most love and care about you is controlling you. You may struggle and go back and forth between what you hope to have with your partner and seeing what is. While you may feel grief and mourn this loss, ultimately you'll feel less confused as you realize what's happening in your relationship. Over time, this will lead to a more confident you.

## Absorb the Truth at a Pace That Works Best for You

You'll gain the most clarity when you are careful not to deny or minimize any part of your experience. I can't stress this enough. Denying and minimizing prevents you from progressing in your recovery, so work on being honest with yourself. At this point in your recovery, it's just you and your experience—you don't need to speak aloud to anyone, certainly not your partner. If you ever have a sense that you weren't entirely honest with yourself at a particular point or while doing an exercise in this book, go back to it. You can redo it. It's likely you will only be able to take in a little information at a time, so slow the pace down or simply put the book away when you need a break. That's okay, your feelings or nervousness are telling you something. Building on what you truly know will help you the most in the end.

Sharon, an artist in her forties, said, "I've tried so hard to change things, to please my husband and hold my family together. But recently, I feel different. I've stopped making excuses for him and begging him to do things. It took me so long to finally get the courage to get started."

Because you're in a recovery process, you can't expect to see and understand everything right away. Try not to be hard on yourself. In time, you'll be in a position to make better choices.

## Begin with What You Already Know

Bringing your feelings into awareness can be a new experience. In stressful situations—like living with a controlling partner—it's common to suppress feelings in order to cope, particularly when it's not safe to express them. However, when you allow your feelings to come into awareness, you will realize that you know what you don't like, what feels unfair, what makes you feel bad, and what scares you. At the same time, doing this brings up feelings that may have also been suppressed, such as feeling disappointed and sad that this is your relationship and your life at the moment.

Women have identified many hurtful actions that their partners have used to control them. While controlling behaviors present themselves quite differently, it's extremely rare that I hear about something and say, "That's not abuse." Actually, this list of behaviors reflects the deep awareness women have of their partner's abuse that, until this point in their recovery, they might not have stopped to take stock of. Harmful actions include:

- accusing me of being crazy or controlling

- blaming me, it's always my fault

- calling me vulgar names like "fucking bitch," "frigid," "cunt," "stupid"

- calling twenty to thirty times a day

- criticizing me constantly

- getting in my face to argue

- making me frightened

- making me show receipts so he knows I went where I said I was going

- ordering me, he tells me what to do

- putting me down in front of the kids and directly to the kids ·

- setting the rules, he can yell but I can't

- spitting in my face

- walking away while I'm speaking

- yelling, swearing, screaming

To compile a list like this can invoke a recognition of abuse. By just asking women to tell me what they believe is abusive in their experience, they quickly identify many things. For many, it's the first time anyone has asked or showed interest in the hurtful behavior that's such a big part of their lives. Perhaps no one, including them, knew what could be done about it.

EXERCISE: Identify Your Partner's Behaviors

In your journal, write down this question: "What behaviors do I suspect are controlling or abusive?" Then list whatever is true for you and let your thoughts and feelings guide you. Be sure to list at least five behaviors—I want you to see that you know more about what's going on than you think you do.

Next, look at the behaviors you listed. Take this moment to appreciate what you know and that you are allowing yourself to recognize your partner's abusive behavior.

When I do this exercise in the recovery groups, I see that at first women are often hesitant to speak aloud about their partners' behaviors. This may be the first time you've faced these behaviors and you may experience many unexpected, even troubling, feelings. Among many reactions, two common ones emerge: feeling disloyal to a partner and distrusting thoughts or perceptions about the abuse. As you do the exercises and learn more, you will eventually resolve the conflict about loyalty and grow to be more confident in your thinking—usually when you can feel indignation at his abuse.

## EXERCISE: Controlling Behavior Checklist

This exercise is adapted from a 1992 domestic violence training document, sponsored by REACH, previously known as the Support Committee for Battered Women. It will allow you to build on the awareness you gained in the last exercise and reflect more deeply on your relationship. As you review the items on the list, you'll get the chance to look at your partner's behavior and to see when your experience with your partner is abusive. Women in recovery groups are often quiet, even somber, as they complete this exercise. It's okay if you feel quieted by this exercise, too. Know that it will help you.

Put a checkmark next to the behaviors you have experienced with your partner. Even if you feel something does not apply, read through and consider all of the controlling behaviors listed. If you experience a behavior you believe is abuse but it's not listed, add it. Perhaps it was something from the previous exercise, when you described his abuse. Remember, all you are doing right now is identifying your partner's controlling behaviors. You don't have to do anything else.

### Psychological Abuse

- [ ] Standing in the doorway during arguments to prevent you from leaving
- [ ] Making angry or threatening gestures
- [ ] Giving you menacing looks
- [ ] Using his body or size to intimidate you
- [ ] Standing over you
- [ ] Shouting you down, exploding, yelling, screaming
- [ ] Driving recklessly to scare you
- [ ] Threatening in many ways, including threatening to take the children away
- [ ] Giving the silent treatment—not speaking or acknowledging you
- [ ] Harassing—seeking you out to annoy you

☐ Stalking you in your home

☐ Using crude language, calling you names

☐ Ridiculing your traits, putting you down

☐ Criticizing your behavior

☐ Blaming you, making false accusations

☐ Using pressure tactics, rushing you into decisions

☐ Making you feel guilty

☐ Manipulating the children

☐ Using your children to coerce you

☐ Interrupting, changing topics, not listening, not responding

☐ Lying, twisting your words, withholding information

☐ Claiming to be the authority, the only one who knows the truth

☐ Controlling your money and making all the financial decisions

☐ Isolating you from family, friends, and neighbors

☐ Preventing you from working outside the home

☐ Sabotaging your job and activities outside your home

☐ Turning family, children, or friends against you

☐ Being jealous, withholding emotionally

☐ Having affairs, infidelity

☐ Calling you constantly to check up on you

☐ Isolating you—making you a prisoner in your own home

☐ Threatening suicide

☐ Threatening to kill you

☐ Threatening abandonment if you don't do what he wants

- [ ] Keeping you up at night with tirades, interfering with your sleep

- [ ] Preventing you from seeking help, whether medical attention or psychotherapy

## Physical Violence

- [ ] Slapping with an open hand

- [ ] Punching with a fist

- [ ] Beating

- [ ] Biting

- [ ] Kicking

- [ ] Dragging

- [ ] Poking

- [ ] Grabbing, yanking arm

- [ ] Twisting arm, squeezing hand

- [ ] Choking, strangling

- [ ] Pushing, shoving

- [ ] Pinching

- [ ] Pulling Hair

- [ ] Physically throwing you

- [ ] Using physical restraints to hold you down, pin you against a wall

- [ ] Throwing objects around

- [ ] Throwing objects at you

- [ ] Spitting on you

- [ ] Abusing furniture, home, your personal possessions

- [ ] Abusing pets

☐  Keeping weapons around that threaten you

☐  Using weapons or objects to threaten you

## Sexual Abuse

☐  Telling jokes against women, objectifying and devaluing you

☐  Degrading you sexually, making you feel ashamed

☐  Using threats or coercion to have sex with you, having sex you don't like

☐  Waking up to find your partner having, or attempting to have, sex with you

☐  Forcing sex acts against your will, raping

Now that you have completed the checklist, take a moment to fully appreciate what you just found out. You're likely to feel surprised, nervous, and upset. These are normal responses. Many women are amazed to discover that many behaviors they didn't consider to be psychological abuse actually are.

By checking a behavior, you have identified your partner's behavior as abusive. You have also moved further out of minimizing and denying. The checkmarks have alerted you to the reality of your intimate relationship.

At the same time, after viewing the controlling behavior checklist, some women express concern that they might be abusive with their partner, too. If you share this concern, go through the checklist and identify your behaviors. Ultimately, none of these behaviors benefit you or your relationship. If you feel you become physically hurtful at times, determine if it's out of self-defense. If it is, then you'd be best served to take steps to get safe and chapter 10 can help. If you identified some of your behaviors as psychological abuse, you need to determine who has the overall power and control in the relationship. If you're clear that it is yourself, then it's in your best interest to seek out help to address your abusive behavior. If you believe it's your partner who chiefly dominates and has primary control in the relationship, then with this book you're in the right place to move forward to receive help and recover.

Next, to better recognize and understand your feelings and responses to what you learned by filling out the controlling behavior checklist, I am providing typical reactions from women in the recovery groups. I believe you'll find them helpful and grounding.

## Common Reactions of Women in Recovery

After identifying your partner's abusive behaviors, you are likely to have many different kinds of reactions. I hope you can find some solace through knowing there is a wide variety of normal responses. Women's initial responses include the following.

### Feeling More Confused

How could this be happening? It's not surprising if you feel confused. You've been exposed to a lot of new information quickly. Also, the knowledge that abuse is happening not only to you, but to other women as well, can be disorienting. In time, as you become clearer, you'll understand the full complexity of what's going on and you'll be glad you are not alone.

### Feeling Scared and Anxious

You have good reason to feel scared and anxious. You've learned that your partner is abusing you and that he does so to gain control over you. You may also be more aware of being in some kind of physical danger. Please take this fear seriously and use the information in chapter 10 to take steps to get safe.

### Feeling Overwhelmed About What to Do

You can certainly feel overwhelmed, given all that you learned. But know that you don't need to do anything right now, unless you want to. You can take your time to thoughtfully figure out what is best for you and this book will help. If you feel you need more support, talk to someone. As you go through your recovery, at any point you can look at the resource section at the end of the book or explore the help available in your community.

## Feeling Shocked

How could he do this to you? How could the most unlikely person, the one from whom you expect caring and love, be abusing you? You can hardly believe it or take it in. You may need more time before you fully comprehend your situation. You will gradually understand more as you move forward.

## Feeling Responsible

You might wonder how you could let this happen. But you've been repeatedly exposed to psychological abuse that's hard to see and develops slowly. Feeling responsible is expected, particularly when you come out of denial. Don't be hard on yourself. As you learn more, you will get clear about how your partner entrapped you.

## Blaming Yourself

Internalizing blame for the abuse is an inherent, traumatic part of being the recipient of abuse. Remember that you are not responsible for his choices, including his abusive behavior.

## Feeling Embarrassed or Ashamed

Shame is a natural response to being hurt, especially by the one you expect to love you. Shame occurs when you think the abuse you endure says something bad about you. For this reason, your shame needs to be addressed as part of your recovery. In time, you'll come to see that it says more about him because he's responsible for his abuse.

## Feeling Numb or Detached

You may feel this way for a while, but in time it is more likely that you will get in touch with your feelings. When you do feel more, you can revisit this list to help you understand your reactions. If you continue to find it difficult to experience your feelings, you might benefit from the help of a counselor or therapist. See the Resource section for recommendations.

## Feeling Irritated or Angry

Your anger may feel terrible, but it's actually a reasonable and healthy response to being abused. Eventually, everyone who is hurt by their intimate partner needs to hold him responsible for his abuse. When you do this, you will naturally feel angry toward the one hurting you. If your feelings are overwhelming and you can't calm yourself, a therapist or counselor can be helpful.

## Feeling Upset and Sad

You may feel this way because you now know what you previously suspected is true. When you finally recognize what is true and get validation, it can feel heartbreaking.

## Feeling Less "Crazy"

You may be glad to know what's going on, although it's hard knowing your partner's behavior is abuse. Knowledge and understanding can be validating and anchoring. This new perspective on your experience can help you feel grounded, which is the beginning of feeling you have some control over your own life.

## Feeling Less Alone

You now know you share this experience with others. When you can identify with other women reading this book and working on their recovery, you feel less alone, and no longer ask, "What is wrong with me? No one else is like this."

## Feeling Relieved Because Your Experience
## Has Been Identified

It starts to make sense. Eventually, all women in recovery get to this place—feeling better from having your experience with your partner validated for what it is—psychological abuse.

Remember, you are learning. This is a big step. You're in a recovery process to get help—similar to a thousand women who came before and those who will follow, including other readers just like you. Know you are not alone.

Now that you have read other women's stories, reflected on your own story, and recognized your partner's behavior as abusive, you may feel stunned by your new awareness and what you have in common with women who have controlling partners. The striking similarities often prompt women to ask, "Why are our partners like this?" Although we'll touch upon this information briefly, I discourage you from focusing on your partner right now. To date, your relationship has been all about him. Your recovery is all about you and what you want going forward. Identifying your goals is a place to start.

# Six Reasons Women Seek Help

Soon you'll set goals for yourself, so I want to share the variety of reasons women seek help and what they hope to achieve in recovery. Some are realistic while some are not. You may see yourself in one or more of the following six reasons.

## To Fix Their Relationship

Women may come to the recovery process to "fix" their relationships, but what they end up learning is how to rescue and restore themselves. Many women believe, and you may too, that they need to speak and act differently so their partner behaves more favorably toward them. If your partner blames you for what "you made him do to you," over time you will end up blaming yourself. Your task is to realize that you are not responsible for his abusive behavior. Women tend to work hard to avoid being hurt or to stop their partners from abusing them, but they aren't successful. You cannot make your partner abuse you and you can't make him not abuse you. These are his choices and his alone. The task is to refocus on yourself and your recovery.

## To Get Stronger

You may know that you are abused and that you no longer want to put up with it. But you may also feel overwhelmed, anxious, confused, or too vulnerable to figure out what to do about your relationship. By recovering and getting stronger, you will be able to protect yourself, figure out what you want, and feel empowered to take the steps to get there. From this position, women are better able to address the abuse with their partner to determine whether he's interested in working on changing.

## To Get Help to Leave

You may have decided to leave your partner but don't know how—or feel able—to do so. The recovery process helps you become emotionally stronger. By completing your recovery, you will be capable and prepared to take steps to leave with plans to do so safely.

## To Deal with the Pressure to Go Back After a Separation

You may have planned your separation from your partner—or it may have been unplanned, something you had to do because he was violent or threatening to harm you. Either way, like many women, you may experience pressure from your partner to get back together. With recovery, you become less vulnerable to giving in to his pressure and more able to keep moving in the direction of what it is you want.

## To Communicate for Co-parenting While Separated or Divorced

If you are separated or divorced, but have shared parenting responsibilities with your ex-partner, you have probably realized you are not any more effective in speaking and negotiating with him now than when you were together. Your recovery will help you stop accommodating him to keep the peace and help you to take a stronger position in which you stay true to your own agenda and concerns. This is particularly important when advocating for the needs of your children.

### To Recover After the Relationship Ended

For some women, the traumatic effects of psychological abuse can linger long after they leave their controlling partners. If this is where you are starting, it is likely you feel afraid, lack trust in your own judgment, and worry about being hurt in future relationships. Your recovery will help you heal, restore your strengths, and become more self-confident to make better choices going forward.

## Make the Commitment to Recovery by Setting Goals

Establishing goals is a commitment, a way to take ownership of your recovery. To set goals at the outset, I ask each woman I work with to decide for herself what is most important for her. By now, I have recorded well over 3,000 personal goals. The goals reveal the deeply felt effects of living with a controlling partner. And as you will see, they then become each woman's hope for her future.

Now is the time to validate your hopes and desires. As you read through the examples of the goals from women in recovery that are offered here, think of how they might be similar to what you want. In your journal, recognize and record those goals that speak to you directly, so you can return to them later when it's time to set your own goals. For now, just know that many women have made progress toward their goals and have reached a better place. And you surely can, too. Goals can include:

- Recognize abuse

- Learn strategies to prevent getting into another controlling relationship

- Figure out whether to stay or leave

- Get over the hurt

- Get stronger and more assertive

- Make a decision about my relationship

- Improve communication with my partner and find better ways to handle conflict

- Raise my self-esteem

- Learn to deal with my husband around contact with the children

- Stand on my own with the children

- Get clear about who I am

- Stand up for myself and find a way to behave, if possible, that will stop him from being abusive

- Make plans for self-care

- Not feel guilty and responsible

- Survive a separation and get on with my life

- Understand why I kept going back and tolerated certain behaviors

- Recover and let go of the past

- Stay focused on what I want for myself

- Get a divorce

- Get strong so as not to get caught in his seduction

- Develop a thoughtful plan to keep moving ahead

- Get my husband out of the house and try to have him leave peacefully

- Feel better and happy

- Get back to my old self

- Learn strategies for dealing with my own responses

- Help him to get help

- Understand my chaotic experience and make sense of it

- Stop being sucked into his control

- Focus on the children

- Stop reacting and let go

- Be less vulnerable to my husband's maneuvers

- Stay strong and not take abuse

- Identify controlling behaviors

- Love myself

- Deal with separation issues

- Find a way to have a healthier life

- Find strategies to maintain a family

- Keep my children and myself safe

Many common themes come up as women state their goals. Here are the three most frequent ones.

## Get Clear About What Is Happening

All women come to realize they need to know what controlling behaviors look like, how these behaviors affect them, and how to respond.

## Become Emotionally Stronger

It is very difficult to make an important decision when you feel confused, are filled with self-doubt, and no longer trust how you see things. Many women don't decide what to do about their relationships until after recovery.

## Feel Like Themselves Again

To feel like yourself again means to no longer feel so fearful, guilty, anxious, and depressed. Women want to re-own the parts of themselves they lost touch with or needed to keep hidden, to start feeling good and confident.

By setting goals, you are saying, "I don't want to live like this anymore." You're identifying how you want things to be. Right now, you most likely don't know how you will make this come about. That's okay. Your goals are for you to work toward. Over time, you'll get clear about how to make changes to improve your life.

### EXERCISE: Identify Your Goals

In your journal, identify your own goals and write them down. There are no right or wrong goals, they can be anything that captures what you want for yourself. Your goals will become your motivation to get to a better place.

What changes would you like to see in your future? If you need to, look at the examples of other women's goals you noted in your journal or return to the list. If you'd like, visualize yourself as a member of a recovery group—imagine being surrounded by the eight or so women who identified their goals to you.

State up to three goals for your recovery. If you'd like, share these goals with a trusted listener. To remind yourself of them as you progress through recovery, revisit your goals from time to time. Near the end of recovery, you will assess the progress you made toward your goals. You will make progress, feel capable of fulfilling the goals in your own time, and benefit from the momentum that sets you well on your way.

## You've Got This!

Your partner's abusive behaviors, which you identified on the Controlling Behavior Checklist, are choices he makes that result in controlling you—abusing you. Your feelings of confusion, guilt, and responsibility for the problems with your partner are all common reactions and are part of the impact of the abuse you endure. When you recognize your experience by owning your story and setting personal goals, you take a big step out of denying and minimizing. Continuing your recovery is the only way to get stronger, protect yourself, and eventually, be free from his control. Once you're in control of you, you decide what you want to do going forward with yourself and your relationship. No one knows what's best for you better than you.

# CHAPTER 4

# Overcoming Powerful External Influences

The last chapter provided a big revelation as you clearly saw your partner's controlling behavior. I believe you deserve a great deal of credit for taking these steps to improve your life. You may not always feel the same way; in fact, you may have mixed feelings. That is completely understandable—the important thing is the part of you that keeps progressing in this process. Take a moment to appreciate that about yourself.

Previously, you identified some of your partner's controlling behaviors. The goals you set in the last chapter provide a window into how you'd like your future to look. In this chapter, you will learn how all women—including you—are made vulnerable to controlling partners by our culture and its influence on the people and institutions that impact your life. At the same time, psychologically abused individuals can feel crazy when society may subtly approve of, or not recognize, their abuse. Before we address this, we look at "why you."

## Why Me?

At this point, the question "Why me?" is often raised. It is an important and common question that needs to be put to rest. Jackie came into one of my groups with the question, "How did I end up with an abusive partner? Why me?" Another woman asked, "Is there something that causes us, in particular, to be abused?" One woman who had suffered through two abusive relationships questioned, "Am I wearing a sign that says 'Abuse me'?"

Similar to many women in controlling relationships, it's likely you're having a hard time making sense of your experience. It's difficult to believe that the person in your life who you turn to for affection and companionship wants to dictate your life and even hurt you to do so. As women struggle to make meaning of this, they often look to themselves for explanations. You may be asking questions like "How did I come to be with a partner who hurts me—who abuses me?" and "What's wrong with me?"

First and foremost, there is nothing about you—absolutely nothing—that justifies abuse. Likewise, there is absolutely nothing about other women that provides a reason for them to be abused. Don't let yourself be convinced otherwise.

Sometimes women believe something is inherently flawed about them and this causes their partner to abuse them. One woman asked the question, "If I felt better about myself, would I then not be abused?" It's important to know that low self-esteem is not the cause for your boyfriend or husband to abuse you—rather it is one of the painful results of being abused. Your partner abuses you not because of you, but because of him and his need to be in control of you—a need often influenced by the culture we live in, as you'll discover in this chapter. Right now, take this in: *You don't deserve to be abused by anyone.*

When your partner blames you again and again, including for his abuse, you can internalize his hurtful accusations to the extent that you believe you are at fault. But your partner is always responsible for his behavior—no matter what you do—and likewise, you are responsible for your behavior. It is inevitable that at times you will say things and act in ways that will trigger other people to get upset, even angry, with you. That's okay. I like to think that, within reasonable bounds, this is our human right. How your partner expresses his anger when reacting to you is entirely up to him. You cannot make someone physically attack you or say terrible things to you.

What you can do is hold your partner accountable for his hurtful actions and verbal assaults. Ultimately, for a controlling partner to change, he needs to genuinely admit to his abuse and believe you are not to blame. This may be very difficult for him to do and, for some, might be impossible.

Janice, a married mother of two school-age children, struggled with this concept of who is responsible for what. She recounted an episode with her husband when she came home after shopping for her children to an onslaught of his rage. Janice admitted that she spent more money on her children's school clothes than she meant to, but clothes had gone up in price. In the store, she believed she made a reasonable decision even as she felt trepidation about her husband's reaction. But she also knew it never mattered whether her decision was reasonable, his issue was always that she decided—not him. For he believes it's his right alone to decide what's best for her and his family. At the time, Janice told herself she would endure whatever happened since the kids needed their school clothes. Besides, she hated seeking his permission, so once in a while she would just refuse to give in to his rules. When her husband found out, he yelled, "You crazy bitch! You're so stupid. You can't even get that right!" He didn't talk to her for days.

Janice had made a decision for which she was responsible. However, even though her decision provoked her husband and made him angry, he had other choices for expressing his anger. He could have simply told her he disagreed with what she did. He could have made the point that, as an adult, she didn't need to seek permission but did need to collaborate with him. There are many ways he could have consciously reacted—but to choose to disagree by yelling at her, degrading her, and punishing her with silence is a deplorable decision. How Janice's partner chose to deal with his reactive anger was abusive and was entirely *his* responsibility.

EXERCISE: **When You Assume Responsibility for Your Partner's Reactions**

With your journal, find a place where you can settle into yourself without distraction. Take a minute to breath calmly. When you're ready, write about situations you have experienced that are similar to Janice's story. The following questions will help you.

- What are some situations that trigger your partner?

- How did you assume, or try to assume, responsibility for your own actions?

- How did your partner respond to your efforts—were you rebuffed?

- What other responses could you imagine your partner having?

- What feelings come up around the idea that you're not responsible for the way your partner reacts to you?

Take some time to review your responses. Keep in mind that it may not be your partner alone who is guilty, it may be the culture at large as well.

## Culture Impacts Your Partner's Controlling Behavior

Although there is nothing inherently wrong with you that would justify abuse, there are external circumstances that can make you, as a woman, more vulnerable to a controlling partner. This can make it harder to protect yourself, receive support, and feel validated.

We live in a culture that generally empowers men more than women, which strongly influences women's lives. The fact that our culture condones men having power over women fuels many controlling partners to dominate and to expect you to be submissive. While many men do not choose this course, the men who do are supported in their actions both implicitly and explicitly because controlling partners exploit culturally reinforced social expectations of women. Although various degrees of progressive change have taken place over time, these social expectations in their extreme form suggest that women be unselfish caregivers who are unassertive and never angry.

At times, this can put you in harm's way as you find yourself going along with ideas and behaviors that do not benefit you. And when you choose to be different from this, you risk being seen as obstinate, wrong, or even crazy. Women can be called a "bitch" for expressing their anger, a "nag" for stating their concerns, or "selfish" for attending to their own needs. It's no coincidence that you find it hard to challenge or change these beliefs because they're intensely reinforced by controlling partners and, at times, even your family and friends. When you question these beliefs for yourself, you will take an important step toward your own empowerment.

Our culture influences how we view men's and women's roles, and how we come to be who we are. Although our culture is one of the most powerful influences, it's not the only one. We all have a unique background with our own personal characteristics, family of origin, and life experiences.

The same cultural conditioning that affects you and your partner also affects your family of origin and friends, community, religious practice, and professionals you contact for help. In turn, these people—who are powerful forces in your life—can reinforce cultural beliefs that do not favor you. The same denial of psychological abuse runs through many layers of influence. If you look at how denial of abuse plays out within your community, institutions, and other influences in your life, you can see that it is harmful to women, particularly to you as a woman with a controlling partner. As you gain clarity and decrease your denial, make sure to have people in your life who truly understand and validate you.

## Family and Friends

Families of origin are where cultural messages get reinforced or discouraged or replaced with other ideas. If demeaning messages about women are strongly reinforced by your family, then it's likely they won't understand your situation, may be harshly critical, and even take your partner's side. This can feel heartbreaking. Even caring family and friends might find it hard to continue their support or understanding because they feel helpless to do anything about your situation. If you are in either of these situations, you might want to find someone who you can trust to support you and talk with you. If you'd like this, look into resources in your area and find a support group. You can continue your recovery using this book, but you'll have added support and a place to share. Check the Resources list at the end of this book for suggestions.

## Community

Abuse exists in all communities and all socioeconomic groups. There's a misperception that only women at the lower end of the socioeconomic range experience domestic abuse. At the middle-to-high end of the socioeconomic range, a greater level of denial exists. When the admissions officer at a hospital in a comfortable suburban community first started asking, "Has someone close to you hurt you physically?" the hospital received complaints. The message from the community can be summed up in this way: "It's appalling to imply that something like this could happen in our town."

When we deny that abuse exists in prosperous communities, we contribute to the hurtful condition by which women, perhaps like yourself, are made vulnerable. If you're a successful, educated woman, you are at risk to be mistakenly viewed as more empowered and therefore unlikely to fall under the abusive control of your intimate partner. Your accomplished partner is often mistakenly seen as not the type to be abusive. Having your harmful experience dismissed in this way can leave you feeling ashamed and pressured to hide the painful reality behind the walls of a seemingly perfect home. If your family members, friends, and neighbors can't believe this could happen to you— someone they know—they might not believe you. In the end, your community may not support you.

## Religious Practice

If you're highly religious, your beliefs may conflict with a growing desire to get out of harm's way. Although some clergy have received domestic violence training, many have yet to do so. Religious affiliations with strong patriarchal influences can contribute the feeling that you have few, if any, options to rectify your situation. However, with some persistence it's becoming more likely you will find help.

Claudia was a devout Catholic, married for seventeen years with four children. She taught religious education every week. As she became aware of her partner's psychological torment and the profound unhappiness that resulted, her despair increased since divorce was unacceptable for "a good Catholic." With her husband's voice and this formidable religious influence in her head, it took Claudia a long time to seek help. With the help of her therapist, eventually Claudia found a priest from another church who understood her pain. He supported her wish to separate because, as he said, "God does not intend for you to suffer in this way." Once she found peace within her faith, Claudia felt empowered to take steps to improve her life and her children's lives. After many attempts, she had to accept that her husband was unwilling to take responsibility for his abuse. In the end, Claudia felt she had no other choice but to divorce her husband.

If you feel pressured by your religious beliefs, take the time to find understanding and supportive people within your religious community. These people will not invalidate or try to control you, but will take your concerns seriously.

## Medical Professionals

In the course of a twenty-one-year marriage, Kyla experienced chronic health issues, including bleeding ulcers and ongoing gastrointestinal problems, and had eight surgeries. Five years after her divorce, she first became aware of the psychological abuse she painfully endured from her spouse and saw how it contributed to her stress-related illnesses. But in all the time she spent with medical professionals, not one doctor or nurse asked about stress or other possible causes of her ailments. If she had been asked, it could have helped her make the connection and, in the end, she could have had far better options than surgeries.

Sensitivity to domestic violence has become a part of the training protocol for nurses and doctors. If you are admitted for medical care in a hospital, clinic, or private practice, they may include questions—usually just one or two—about whether someone is hurting you. When you answer these questions, keep in mind that your hurt may not be the result of physical abuse. Even conditions that seem unrelated may be the result of psychological abuse. Primary care physicians, nurse practitioners, and nurses—who make it their business to know about psychological abuse and the related physical and mental health conditions—will be the best resource for you. Find out if your medical care professionals are trained in domestic violence and understand psychological abuse so that they can help you. Expect no less. When your medical professionals are prepared to offer understanding, give you information, and suggest resources, they can provide a life-changing intervention.

## Legal System

Law enforcement officers, lawyers, judges, or a *guardian ad litem* (the person appointed by the courts to represent the best interest of a child) have a tremendous impact on the lives of women with controlling partners. Whether they are helping with issues of safety, divorce, or child custody, they all need to be knowledgeable about abusive experiences and be open to you. While the legal system currently recognizes physical abuse and not psychological abuse, it is possible to receive judicious legal support and judgment. In Stage Three and also in this book's Resources section, I provide more information.

## Mental Health Professionals

More women who suffer from psychological abuse turn to mental health professionals for help than to domestic violence organizations, shelters, or phone hotlines. Because they feel emotionally unwell and experience depression, anxiety, or trauma, they seek out a type of therapy they believe can help with these symptoms. Or, since their relationship is in trouble, they might look to couples therapy—which is not always the best option for controlling relationships. When you haven't been hit, you don't think of yourself as a victim of domestic violence. Unfortunately, many therapists are unprepared to help their patients identify coercive behavior and psychological abuse because they don't recognize or understand it. Years of couples therapy can be wasted because a social worker, psychologist, or other mental health professional did not take the steps to become educated about the unique treatment issues for women enduring abuse. Too often, I hear women describe a course of treatment that failed to make a difference.

Emily, a thirty-two-year-old woman, found her way to a group after years of trying to get help through couples therapy, with no success. She told the group that the therapist put the onus on her to make the relationship work. The therapist counseled her to avoid making her husband angry and to be more understanding of, and sensitive to, his neglectful and abusive childhood. Of course, Emily's efforts never worked. Her self-blame intensified and she became more confused and depressed. The therapist never held her husband accountable for his angry, controlling behavior, which made him feel more justified in blaming and abusing her. In the end, the therapist failed them both.

Your mental health treatment is only effective when it addresses the unvarnished truth of the problem—that abuse is not a shared responsibility. Couples therapy may not be the first treatment of choice here. Mental health professionals who are uninformed and unprepared will not be aligned with what you need to truly be helped. I'll go into more detail about this in chapter 14.

## Your Anger Tells You What You Don't Like

Our culture does not encourage women to be angry or openly express anger, like it encourages men. And women often feel responsible for making a relationship work. As a result, women are prone to suppressing and internalizing anger—which leads to depression and anxiety. No wonder women experience a much higher rate of depression than men (Kiecolt-Glaser and Newton 2001; Bird 1999; Lynch 1988), and that rate is even higher among married women. In controlling or abusive relationships, expressing yourself—especially your anger—is unwelcome and even unsafe. You may hear accusations like "You're the controlling, abusive one!" But know that, in the end, it's your ability to feel anger that will help save you. You can then choose whether to express it and how—but first, at least acknowledge it within yourself.

Pam, a thirty-year-old married woman, felt her anger and stood up for herself by expressing it. Unfortunately, her anger was unacceptable to her husband—as it would be for any controlling partner. One morning, while rushing around the kitchen making coffee and breakfast before heading to work, Pam managed to get around her husband, who had stiffly planted himself in front of the dishwasher. In a menacing tone, he started in on her: "You never get this right. You just throw the damn dishes in. How many times do I have to tell you how to do it? You need to fix this mess now!"

Pam had heard this complaint again and again. She tried to accommodate him but with their busy lives, just getting the dishes in there was a wonder. Sometimes she felt upset, but this was one of those times her husband's demeaning attitude seemed so uncalled for that she couldn't help but express her anger—loud and clear. Hearing his "order" for the fifth time, she reacted strongly: "Get off my back! I've been busy. Besides, the dishes will get clean anyway. If you don't like it, fix it yourself!"

Her husband shouted back, "Look at you, bitch! You're out of control. Look what else I have to put up with!" The expectation to not be angry or express anger puts women like Pam in terrible conflicts. From experiences like this, Pam knew nothing good would ever come from expressing her anger to her husband. Pam never felt taken seriously—no matter how she explained the cause of her anger or how loud she got. Since her husband believed she had no right to be angry with him, he used her anger to justify his abuse. At the same time, he made himself out to be the victim of unfair treatment from Pam, which is a common position for controlling partners to take. Pam always ended up feeling badly and believing she did something terribly wrong by getting angry. This made her susceptible to believing her partner must be right. When Pam blamed herself, her husband avoided responsibility for his abuse and she continued to be under the thumb of his control.

Pam grew up in a family that allowed anger to be expressed. But her husband blamed her anger for his reaction saying, "If you didn't get so bitchy, I never would have gotten mad like that." Over time, Pam became more confused and less able to sort out reasonable anger from unreasonable anger, and mostly ended up feeling wrong.

During her recovery, Pam was able to see her anger as reasonable and important to feel—other women in the group even envied her for being able to get angry. Pam's anger wasn't out of control, as her husband said. Her husband's accusation deflected attention from his own menacing behavior. Pam came to realize that when she believed her husband's accusation, she disempowered herself. In time, Pam came to trust in herself more, including in her angry feelings.

## EXERCISE: Getting to Know Your Anger

Here are four statements that reveal an attitude toward feeling and expressing anger. Record how often the response fits with your experience. Is it true "rarely or never," "sometimes," "often," or "very often"?

- I'm not aware of being angry.

- I believe it's okay to be angry, but I have difficulty feeling it.

- I can feel angry at times, but don't feel it's okay to express it.

- I feel intense anger that erupts and overwhelms me.

Now look at your responses. If you answered "often" or "very often," you're in a position to work on your anger, which is the feeling that lets you know that something is not right.

At the same time, anger that erupts in ways that overwhelm you does not help you in any way and its roots can be identified and addressed in individual counseling or therapy.

To let yourself feel anger is a difficult task given both the cultural messages we have explored and your partner's hurtful ways of handling his anger. It's important for you to know that your anger, when you can let yourself feel it, lets you know what you don't like, what feels unfair, and what hurts you. Perhaps you're beginning to feel some irritation or frustration toward your partner as you learn about his controlling ways. It's necessary to experience your anger in order to feel stronger and more empowered. Anger energizes you and helps you to be assertive—in whatever way you choose. Begin by just letting yourself feel your anger. You don't need to express it until you want to and, certainly, you don't need to express your anger the way your partner expresses his.

# Being Assertive by Speaking Up for Yourself

Speaking up for yourself and being assertive isn't always well received, and is certainly not encouraged by a controlling partner. When women speak up about things their controlling partners don't want to hear, they risk being criticized, put down, ignored, or called a nag. They'll likely try again, as people often do when they are ignored and not heard, especially if what they're talking about is important to them. Their partners react even more negatively, which devalues their experience and intimidates them to discourage them from speaking up any further. The message is, "If you express yourself, you're asking for it." So you learn to keep things to yourself.

I was facilitating my third recovery group when the news broke that O.J. Simpson had been found "not guilty" for the murder of his wife. The women described their husbands' reactions to the verdict. Four of the seven women reported that their partners claimed, in more or less the same words, "She must have been really nagging him (asking for it) that day!" Understandably, the women in the recovery group were shocked and astounded by their partners' statements. One woman exclaimed, "How outrageous to blame the dead woman." Another said, "Look how far they'll go with blaming their partner. Now that's scary." In the end, the women each decided their husband's judgment was frightening and not right. As a result, they gave less credence to their partner's view and clearly saw that blaming is unfair. This helped them take a leap in valuing their own perspective.

## EXERCISE: Asserting Yourself

These questions will help you see just how silenced you feel in your relationship. How often do these things happen? Is it "rarely or never," "sometimes," "often," or "very often"?

- When you take up a concern with your partner, do you feel anxious or fearful?

- Does your partner imply you're nagging or giving him a hard time to justify his reaction or ridicule of you?

- Do you stay silent about your concerns in order to avoid the pain of enduring his response?

If your responses were chiefly "often" and "very often," you can see how your partner's hurtful, devaluing comments are intended to humiliate and shame you. They work in powerful ways to discourage you from speaking your concerns. Eventually, to overcome your partner's control, you will need to believe you are not complaining or nagging but that you are a woman with the right to speak up—many times if necessary—to be heard.

## Taking Care of Yourself

Like most women, do you have a strong aversion to being seen as selfish? Since being selfish is so counter to caregiving—the quality that our culture has come to prize above all others in women, you might feel deeply hurt by such an accusation. When you're partnered with someone controlling, the belief that taking time for yourself is selfish can be used against you. Over time, it only becomes harder to overcome.

Bess, a young mother, shared that she constantly carried her spouse's demeaning, contemptuous tone with her since he called her selfish—no matter what she did or didn't do. He called her selfish if: instead of getting her husband what he wanted that minute, she took time to finish a task on the computer; she took the kids out to play rather than being with him; she cooked something that wasn't his favorite meal; she expressed a desire that didn't mirror his. For Bess, this wounding attack went deep since her mother told her the same thing growing up—something she had shared with her spouse early in their relationship.

Bess shared the confusion and shame being called selfish aroused and explored what she thought it meant about her. In reality, the choices she made for herself and her kids were not selfish at all. Her husband used the description when he wasn't getting what he wanted. Bess was being a good mother to take her kids out to play and a responsible person when she finished her tasks on the computer. With this view, she saw that acting in the best interests of herself and her children did not mean she was selfish. Bess learned she had a right to do what she was doing and that it didn't make her selfish. She realized that her husband was using her vulnerability from the past to get her to do what he wanted.

Does your partner demand your attention and time, accusing you of being selfish when you're not accommodating? Do you give in to him to avoid his wrath and being seen as selfish? If so, there is a metaphor I'd like you to keep in mind. When traveling by airplane, just before takeoff, the airline attendant instructs passengers that if you're traveling with children, you should put your own oxygen mask on first and then put one on your child. Your recovery is like putting the mask on yourself first. In reality, you can take care of yourself and also give to others. Your self-care can even make you a better caregiver.

EXERCISE: Do a Reality Check

With cultural messages and your partner's attempts to coerce you to his way of thinking, you can benefit from the input of an outside source that can counter your partner's perspective. His view has governed your life, influencing the way you see things. If you have someone in your life you trust or can find someone, I strongly encourage you to do a "reality check." Share your perspective with someone you trust and ask, "Does what I'm thinking make sense to you?" Ask in any way that feels comfortable to you. Inquiring helps you to receive feedback like, "Yes, that makes perfect sense." Reality checks help you to feel grounded and work toward developing trust in your own judgment again.

# Marriage Is Not a Vow to Endure Abuse

In our culture, marriage can come with old, traditional expectations. In a marriage—even one in which the wife is a stay-at-home mom—no spouse should forfeit her rights or liberties in the relationship. When a couple agrees on a division of labor and household responsibilities, both sides can respect what the other brings to the relationship and family. When this works, the couple shares power and a healthy relationship. But when one person seeks power over the other, it fails miserably.

Lois, a married and at-home mother in her forties, decided to attend a recovery group shortly after her husband was laid off. She reported that he made her life at home increasingly unpleasant, difficult, and even outright scary. Day in and day out, he watched her and stalked her in the house, following on her heels from room to room. When she prepared dinner, folded clothes, or tried to watch television, he stood nearby and made disparaging remarks. "Your meals are like you—tasteless." "Go ahead and do the laundry, fold clothes—it's all a show. You can't keep up with anything. Look at this house, what a mess!" Sometimes she got out of the house to escape his torment, only to return to being ruthlessly interrogated about where she went and what she did. Her explanations never satisfied him. His constant psychological abuse eventually became more menacing and included throwing a fork at her, breaking a plate near her, and preventing her from leaving a room.

Lois shared that she enjoyed being at home, raising children and taking care of domestic responsibilities. She didn't mind having her husband be in charge of the finances and making major decisions for the family. That was how she grew up—it was familiar and comfortable. For quite a while, this seemed to work well for her. However, when her husband lost his position, he became upset and angry, and took it out on her. As he escalated the intensity of his abuse, her life and sense of well-being deteriorated. She went from having time alone to pursue interests to being criticized constantly about tasks she had performed well for years. She felt she could no longer do anything right. Lois lived in a state of fear and anxiety, on high alert for her husband's next attack.

As Lois learned about controlling partners, she came to recognize that her husband had been psychologically abusive, albeit infrequently, for a long time before he lost his job. She eventually understood that he projected his feelings of incompetence from losing his job onto her, making her out to be the failure. Ultimately, through her recovery work, Lois gained strength and decided to stay with her husband on the premise that he'd change his hurtful behavior. He sought help and they succeeded in having a relationship of mutual respect.

## You've Got This!

Because of cultural influences through institutions and people, it can take longer for some women to seek help or to follow through with recovery. Do not let these influences deter you from your course. Remember that you are not alone, for other women like you are taking steps to learn and heal from the hurtful experience of a controlling partner.

The culture and its powerful influences can make you feel misunderstood and vulnerable. But, in the end, it's your partner who hurts you and who is the only one responsible for his abuse. In the next chapter, you'll look at your dating experience as the beginning of Stage Two of your recovery. Looking at how you came to be with your partner is a way to start getting out from under his control.

STAGE TWO

# Deconstruct What Holds You Captive— Breaking Free

# CHAPTER 5

# Dating: What You Didn't Know About His Behavior

Now that you've completed Stage One, take a moment to praise yourself for what you've accomplished. You achieved awareness of your partner's controlling behavior, started to recognize it as psychological abuse, and learned that to blame yourself for the abuse is the result of being abused.

To enter Stage Two, you're staying with the recovery process even though I imagine this feels unsettling, stressful, maybe even scary. At the same time, you have a lot to gain by knowing more because it puts you in the best position to help yourself and your relationship. In the stage of recovery offered in this chapter, you'll examine the period when you and your partner first came together. Your controlling partner is the most powerful force that impacts you in many adverse ways—and it all started when the two of you were dating.

## Courtship and Coercive Persuasion

Courtship is defined as that early period when two people meet with the purpose of developing a romantic relationship that could lead to marriage (Merriam-Webster 2016). Although the word is not commonly used these days, the experience of courtship still applies to our relationships. Since courting behavior is created with the intent to persuade someone to develop a romantic relationship, it can also reveal the early warning signs of a controlling partner.

Women with controlling partners, unbeknownst to them, are frequently entrapped during the time they begin dating. While you may be seeking a meaningful connection with a person, a controlling partner is looking for someone he can gain power over. You may not know or suspect it, but while you are getting to know him, he is getting to know the ways that he could use to later attain control over you. In essence, your heart is open, but your eyes don't see what he doesn't want you to see.

Of course, you may recall pleasant and exciting times with your partner at the beginning, filled with fun, kindness, and closeness. You likely experienced what many women report during courtship: being attended to, listened to, complimented, cared for, trusted, and encouraged. In fact, one of the challenges you now face may be that your dating experience was not out of the ordinary and was more or less what one might expect. If your experience with your partner was favorable in many important ways, it contributed to feeling closer. In fact, most of the women with an abusive partner initially had enough positive encounters with their partner to make it reasonable to forge ahead with a committed relationship.

During the dating period, a controlling partner deliberately maneuvers to win over the one he seeks out. He might choose to be on his best behavior and not show controlling tendencies to look good. For example, he might let a woman make all the decisions while dating—where to go and what to do. He might reduce his controlling tendencies to make his behavior appear closer to what he imagines she will be receptive to. He might display some coercive behaviors to ascertain how she reacts to him, which lets him know more about how to influence her. What is most telling about a controlling partner's behavior during the courtship is that it changes once a commitment is made.

Carla thought Jason's marriage proposal after six months of dating felt too fast. Yet she went ahead and married him anyway. They had met at a professional conference and the physical attraction was quite strong from the start. During the first few months she loved how inseparable they were, spending all their time together seeing movies, enjoying dinners out, and just talking. She felt that he really listened to her, that she could tell him about her hurtful past and see compassion in his eyes. He always did what he said he would do, picking her up on time and following through with the plans they made. It felt wonderful to have someone so attentive and dependable. The attention he showered upon her even impressed her friends. Carla said it felt great to be with Jason then; she had come to believe he was "the love of her life."

In her recovery, it was important for Carla to learn that she couldn't have expected herself to know something about her partner that he intentionally prevented her from seeing. The wonderful, whirl-wind romance prevented her from seeing him fully and its deception convinced her that he was the right guy for her. When he proposed after only six months, even though it felt premature and she felt pres-sured, she jumped for the wonderful life she imagined. She was con-vinced she had every right to plan a future with him. It wasn't until after they married that she saw other parts of him—his anger, jealousy, and possessiveness—that came to constrain her life.

Carla later learned that by persuading her to commit after a brief dating period, Jason put her at risk of being controlled from the start. She didn't take the time she needed to truly know Jason beyond the initial infatuation. She didn't take the time to ask herself these key questions:

- Why is he in such a rush to get married?

- Can I raise my concerns about the timing without worrying about his reaction?

- Do I see him as someone I can negotiate with about impor-tant matters like getting married?

- Why don't I trust my own judgment about the quickness of the proposal?

Controlling partners can appear strong, sensitive, and focused in their wooing behavior—almost too good to be true—while revealing few signs of controlling or abusive tendencies. In all the descriptions of dating relationships collected from women in the recovery groups, most women experience very little control. If a partner's controlling behavior is detected, women tend to ascribe it to something other than psychological abuse. The courtship period is the time we're "falling in love" —and it's natural to minimize or ignore some irritating traits, especially when the positive experience is far more compelling. What is disconcerting and ultimately dangerous is when the irritating traits or behaviors are not seen or understood as psychological abuse. In this case, the "falling" in love can lead to a very treacherous tumble.

## When Signs Are There, But You Can't See Them

When signs of coercive behaviors are present during dating, women who don't know enough about them can't recognize them as abusive.

Denise met Nick at the beginning of her senior year in college. Their attraction was intense, and when they weren't in class they studied together or just hung out. Denise described Nick as fun, with a great sense of humor that made him generally well-liked. She enjoyed his romantic attention: he gave her flowers, played her favorite music, and paid careful attention to her needs during sex. The only times she remembers not being comfortable with Nick was when they disagreed and, at first, this happened only rarely.

Denise recalled that initially he would become irritable and say something to her that felt mildly unpleasant. When that occurred, she mostly felt confused. Eventually, he would resort to outright criticism. Finally, his disgust at her point of view during a confrontation progressed to a point at which he wouldn't say anything at all—only sneer. After that, each time she saw the sneering look, she felt uneasy and became quiet. He would take this as a sign that she had given in, so he became lovingly engaging again.

Soon enough, Denise avoided these moments by not saying what she thought, and over time Denise paid more attention to his needs—not realizing this came at the expense of her own. Yet she loved Nick and could only say yes when he suggested living together after graduation.

Unlike Carla's experience, Denise's courtship provided tangible signs of trouble, yet she overlooked them. Conflict inevitably occurs in all relationships and a lover's quarrel here or there does not necessarily signal trouble. What matters is how a couple handles these moments of conflict and how your partner responds when you express your point of view. A controlling partner will find ways to intimidate you into silence or can punish you if you go against him. He won't accept, or even want to listen to, opinions that differ from his own, as a loving partner would do. If you avoid conflict, you will never find out how your partner reacts to having differences and resolving them. If you put up with behavior that harms you—as Denise tolerated Nick's hurtful behavior—the situation is likely to only get worse.

Denise learned that avoiding conflict with Nick had serious ramifications. At the first signs of conflict, she reacted by feeling unsure, then becoming anxious, intimidated, and eventually completely quiet. While these reactions avoided conflict, they also made her vulnerable. She missed two big signs of control: Nick's negative reactions to her opinions and the intimidating looks that silenced her.

After seeing all this laid out through her work in the recovery group, Denise decided to seek individual therapy to learn how to deal with conflict. When ready, she planned to tell Nick that unless he took responsibility for his hurtful behavior and sought help to make lasting changes, she would not stay with him.

Although Nick was controlling, Denise made herself vulnerable by not standing up for herself because of her fear of conflict. Later, in Stage Three, you'll learn more about how personal issues, like avoiding conflict, leave you vulnerable to a controlling partner.

## Seeing All the Signs

If you're in a committed relationship, such as marriage or living together, then looking back will help you understand how you may have come to be with a controlling partner. If you are currently dating, might get back into dating soon, or have turned to this book in the aftermath of a relationship with a controlling partner, now is the time to examine your experience. This is not a time to be critical of yourself, but instead to be open to how you came to be with your partner so it can make sense to you.

Looking at what women from the recovery groups identified in their courtships may help you realize how controlling partners—including your own—present themselves. It will also prepare you for the work you'll do with your own relationship. This list shows that the courtships had many positive traits with fewer negative ones, although the negatives were strongly felt. The danger lies in not seeing the behaviors as signs of a partner who has the potential to be controlling. As you look over this list, record in your journal the behaviors that describe the experience of your partner while you were dating. Asterisks indicate behaviors that show clear signs of controlling behavior, although at the time may not have been recognized as such.

- He was compassionate, kind, helpful, polite, and well-mannered
- He had a strong family background
- He took charge and was confident
- He gave me wonderful gifts that swept me off my feet*
- He was trustworthy, well-educated, and respected by others
- I felt cared for and loved
- He called me all the time, many times a day*
- He helped me feel good about myself
- He wanted us to have privacy*
- We had good communication, he talked and also listened
- He was interested in who I am—we made decisions together
- He was open to my friends and shared his friends
- He was passionate—sex was off the charts
- He kept his friends away, which made me suspicious*
- He wasn't always interested in me, as he had other interests
- I could be more myself with him
- He was generous with his time, money, and attention
- I looked to him to take the lead while dating, which felt okay since I was falling in love
- My family liked him and he liked my family
- He deferred to me, I made most of the decisions*

- He was respectful but also could be distant

- He was always there, he would just show up*

- We shared ideals and dreams and planned for the future

- He came on strong when he proclaimed his love and won me over*

- His jealousy made me feel special*

- His direction and advice felt positive

- He made me feel guilty for seeing people and doing things without him*

- He made his possessiveness out be my problem*

- He was supportive and always said, "We'll get through it"

- He was adoringly romantic

- I did more of what he wanted to do to keep the peace*

- He seemed so stable, I thought, *I can trust him*

- I felt he would take good care of me

- I spent time with his friends, but never my friends*

- We spent a lot of time alone together, which felt okay since I didn't want to share him

- During conflicts, he would threaten to end the relationship so I gave in*

## What You See May Not Be What You Ultimately Get

Some of these descriptions hardly seem to apply to someone who is abusive. But I've seen time and again that these very positive characteristics and experiences contribute to a women's choice to stay involved, develop a relationship, and then commit to a future with their partner. However, these powerful influences during the dating period can result in being "taken captive by courtship."

Your potential partner may be kind and caring in a number of ways. He may be communicative and even supportive of your interests and work. If some irritating or negative qualities reveal themselves, you might overlook them—especially when you do not see them as signs of a much larger, serious problem. If your prospective partner's behaviors bothered you, he might have convinced you that he's not really like that or that he will change. Unfortunately, the women in support groups came to believe in an image of their partner that didn't hold up over time, as a positive image can be a calculated move. Furthermore, the women missed warning signs that can shout "control." After completing their recovery, these controlling tendencies became clear. Here are some examples of the most egregious controlling behaviors, as they appear during dating.

## Elaborate Gifts

If you receive elaborate gifts, dinners, or vacations that seem excessive since you do not know one another well, be suspicious. One woman learned from the reaction of other women in her recovery group how inappropriate it is to receive an expensive gold bracelet on a second date. She had been so distracted by the attention and how special she felt that she didn't see his lavish gift as a part of a tactic to win her over.

## Isolation

If your partner finds ways for the two of you to always be alone, he's likely isolating you. This can take different forms that we'll address in chapter 8. One woman said that she felt it was very romantic when her boyfriend always wanted to be just with her. But as the relationship went on, she came to realize it was because he was jealous and possessive.

## Few or No Friends

If your partner is not social, has few or no friends, or does not want you to meet his friends, then take this seriously. The woman who became suspicious of her partner when he wouldn't share his friends turned out to be right: he was not comfortable socially and did not support her in being social. Like her, you may not always understand your gut feeling, but try to trust it.

### Frequent Calls and Visits

If your partner calls a lot and visits without invitation, then take his behavior as controlling. The women who experienced this felt flattered and relieved to not have to wait around wondering, "Will he call?" Even though they were made to feel special, the women realized in hindsight that the attention was not what it seemed to be.

In the future, if any of these behaviors show up you will know to examine the situation further for other signs of control.

## Looking at Your Own Dating Experience

In this chapter, we identified the dating period as a time when your partner can conduct himself in ways that reveal very few, if any, indications of his tendency to control. To understand just how you got where you are, it helps to make sense of how you came to be with your partner. Like the women in the recovery groups did, identify his behaviors during your dating period. If you're dating someone presently, make a list of what's currently happening with your boyfriend. Feel free to draw on the list of behaviors offered by other women earlier in the chapter.

### EXERCISE: Your Dating Experience

For this exercise, respond to the following questions in your journal.

- What qualities did your partner have at the outset of your relationship?

- What impressed you?

- Did he do anything that felt uncomfortable or that upset you?

- Were there characteristics or behaviors in him that you found less favorable, yet tolerable given the positive aspects of the relationship?

- Were you confused by any of his behavior?

- If you experienced negative behavior, did he apologize and make his behavior seem like an isolated incident?

After you finish the exercise, look over your responses. As you make meaning out of your experience with your partner, focus on the positive reasons you went ahead with the relationship.

If you discover glaring evidence of controlling behavior, but you forged ahead anyway, then there might have been other factors at play that made you accept him. These can include the cultural influences we looked at in Stage One or it can include your past—which, as you'll learn in Stage Three, can make you more susceptible to a controlling partner. Whatever convinced you to stay with him, know the abuse is not your fault—that will always belong to him.

You will recognize that, for the most part, there were good reasons you decided to be with your partner. Perhaps there were no negative signs whatsoever. But if you did perceive signs of control, it is likely that you experienced one or more of the following responses that led you to continue the relationship. Look these over and decide what was true for you. During your dating period, you may have:

- Missed warning signs by misinterpreting your partner's intentions

- Ignored controlling behaviors because of the compellingly positive aspects of your relationship

- Believed his behavior was an isolated incident

- Believed you could help him to change

- Felt uncertain, but did not trust your instincts or judgment

- Been made vulnerable to accepting unkind behavior because of your past

- Not known how to identify psychological abuse

Whatever the explanation, you need to understand how you came to be with your partner and recognize that, at the time, you did the best you could.

# Time for a Check-In

In the groups, the women "check in" with themselves to recognize how they are doing. Here, I would like you to take a moment to check in with yourself. At this point, you could be having a couple of reactions. Perhaps what you've learned so far has stirred strong feelings of disbelief, hurt, sadness, embarrassment, shame, or even anger. Like Carla, you may feel self-critical and be asking yourself, "How did I let this happen?" or "Why did I let it continue?" These feelings are all understandable, even expected, and shared by many women. The more you know and understand, the more you can stop blaming yourself and seek inner peace. Knowing leads to confidence and the ability to protect yourself in the future.

# You've Got This!

During the dating period, controlling partners often do not show their controlling or abusive tendencies. If they did, most likely you did not see their behavior as psychological abuse. In the next chapter, we look at how a relationship with a controlling partner picks up speed after you have made a commitment to one another.

CHAPTER 6

# From Dating to Commitment to Confinement

In chapter 5, you looked at your dating period and how you came to be with your partner. You're learning how your partner's attention during courtship appeared caring yet started a subtly seductive, coercive arrangement. Take a moment to give yourself credit for your growing awareness and appreciate what you've accomplished so far.

In this chapter, you'll see that when you commit to a future together, your partner's controlling nature can either show up in earnest or develop slowly as an insidious influence that takes over your life.

## After Commitment, a Controlling Partner Takes More Control

When you commit to a controlling partner, he transforms and not for the better. What your partner learned about you in the courtship phase, including your vulnerabilities, helps him influence and persuade you after you commit—whether that means moving in together or getting married. He saw your growing interest in him as assurance that you wouldn't easily leave him. What may have felt like an enjoyable, comfortable partnership starts to insidiously erode your autonomy as he takes more control. If you had easy communication and interactions during dating, you'll experience their slow fade. As he gains more power, a relationship that previously embraced you both becomes more and more "all about him."

In time, your controlling partner shows more interest in his beliefs and needs. If he paid attention to your feelings during dating, he doesn't now or does far less often. If he would pay attention, he would see that you are upset or hurt and he would adjust his behavior. Instead, he doesn't show concern for your feelings or make a genuine attempt to change. At this point, you start to see his true intentions emerge.

# Moments of Understanding

Many women report that it was during this period, when relationships went from dating to commitment, that their lives gradually—or suddenly—changed. Their stories of when they first noticed their partner's control or abuse can help you see how tactics common to controlling partners become evident. As you will see, what captured their attention was most often an obvious and extremely upsetting, hurtful episode of abuse.

### He Isolates You

"Shortly after getting married, we moved from Pennsylvania to Oregon for a new job, and I left behind my family and friends. I felt I had little say in the decision but told myself it had to happen because it was for his work and I didn't want to start my marriage by refusing to go. In a short time, I found myself very isolated. He started restricting my calls and made it hard for me to access money to go out."

### He Devalues You

"After the birth of our daughter, he changed. He gradually shifted away from paying attention to what was important to me to emphasizing his interests only. He made decisions that disregarded my feelings and concerns. The most painful memory I have is pleading with him to let my parents see their new granddaughter and being completely ignored. When he finally decided to let my parents see her, ten months had passed since her birth. I felt so betrayed, but still somehow wondered if I had caused him to treat me so badly."

## He Intimidates You

"The first time I saw his anger escalate was during our honeymoon. We were on a Caribbean island, driving to the beach on a beautiful day. I was in a glowing daze listening to reggae music with my eyes closed. Suddenly, his voice boomed, 'Fuck you!' Now wide-awake, I watched him tailgate and shout obscenities at a driver he said passed too close to us. When I asked him to slow down, he ignored me. I asked again and told him that he was scaring me. He continued raging, but it was turned on me. He started with, 'What the hell do you know? You're giving me a hard time when the other driver started it. Lay off!' On and on he went—in a flash, he had become a maniac. I couldn't believe he was the person I just married."

## He Financially Coerces You

"After getting married, my partner decided how to spend our money. He expected to pay for everything essential with my income alone. When it came the extras, he could always buy a new golf bag, but I never had the freedom to buy new shoes. His frequent, menacing looks became so intimidating that I was too afraid to spend money or ask for things."

Some controlling partners will push a woman into a marriage commitment, believing she is less apt to give up on the relationship and leave him. When relationships become committed, and a partner's control increases, women can more easily notice their discomfort with their partner's behavior. This is the time when control that once was subtle becomes more obvious and what occurred infrequently now happens more often.

EXERCISE: Your Moment of Understanding

In your journal, respond to the following prompts.

- When was the first time you noticed your partner's control? Describe what took place.

- Was it subtle, such as a switch in how your partner spoke to you? Did you get a clipped response that showed irritation? Did he ignore you, offering no response at all? Or was it more overt, such as a financial takeover or putting you down?

- When did the transition occur? How soon after forming a commitment? If it happened to be during the dating period, then describe that.

- What was your initial reaction?

- Did you speak up or overlook it? If you spoke up, what happened? If you overlooked it, what was your reason for doing so?

## His Control Started with Small Exploits

Your controlling partner uses mental and emotional pressure to push you toward what he believes and wants. At first, your partner may have started controlling you by exploiting a small difference that exists between you.

Reflecting back, Brenda still feels amazed at how charming her husband was while they were dating. "He was attentive and engaging—I loved the way he made me feel. How could I not feel loved, not feel admired? When I fell in love and he proposed, it seemed perfect. But now, I hate to think about my marriage. It's so hard to be reminded that the person who claimed to love me eventually hurt me the most."

While they were dating, Brenda's husband never mentioned his feelings about the fact that she had not completed college. But once they were married, her lack of a degree became his first big target. "Once he had me, I painfully learned how he really felt. He told me that I was an embarrassment to him. He was a professional with a PhD and I was a high-school graduate still working on my college degree. His long verbal tirades—about me being stupid, uneducated, and low-class—lasted into the night. They were his way to beat me down, show me just how worthless I am and how great he is. Eventually, I came to believe it."

Not long after getting married, Brenda became the recipient of brief yet demeaning comments such as, "How would you know? That's stupid" and "You don't know what you're talking about." Once a partner gets hold of a vulnerable edge, as Brenda's husband did when he discovered how insecure she felt about the difference in their education, he builds on this to create a shift in power. He repetitively uses more coercion and, if necessary, increases the severity—as Brenda's husband did by subjecting her to nightly tirades of intense ridicule, put downs, and intimidation. But less intense abuse can still achieve the same result.

Eventually, your partner dominates you, at your expense. You feel beaten down, confused, and vulnerable, which makes it harder for you to resist his control. Any time there's a threat to his power, your partner exerts abuse to get back in control again. Each time he is coercive, the next time can be a little more intense. He gradually builds his power to take control in your relationship. To you, your partner's controlling behavior may appear random, but he has a clear agenda.

## EXERCISE: How Did His Control Show Up?

To expand on the previous exercise, identify what changes in his behavior started to show up more often. At first, you may not have noticed your partner's coercive agenda, but you may have sensed subtle changes. With your journal, document as much as you can in response to these questions.

- Did he begin to criticize you about things that never seemed to bother him before?

- Did he stop following through with things that were important to you?

- Did he stop showing interest in what you like or stop supporting you altogether?

- Have you found that it's no longer okay to go out with friends or pursue your own interests?

- Did his control show up around money?

As you examine the transition when he was becoming more and more controlling, it's important to identify how you reasoned with yourself so you could move on in the relationship. These questions apply to what you did then and also to what you might continue to do in order to cope and move on with your partner after an abusive episode.

- Were you confused by his behavior, so you let it go or felt unable to address it?

- Did he apologize for his behavior, with you accepting his apology?

- Did he make his behavior out to be an isolated incident that wouldn't happen again and you chose to believe him?

- Did you feel responsible, so you decided to try harder in the future to get things right?

List anything else that feels relevant. Take a moment to review your responses. Start to see how his control unexpectedly seeped into your life.

## Upping the Intensity

In time, money became the biggest sticking point in Brenda's marriage—and her husband's most effective tool for controlling her. Early on in their marriage, her husband embarked on a campaign of mental pressure so she would give in to him regarding money matters. Since he was more educated and made more money, he told her that he would decide how money is spent. He used what he believed to be his "intellectual superiority" to make the claim that he would manage their money because "I know best," thus keeping Brenda financially dependent. Brenda had to rely on an inadequate allowance for herself and their two young children. When she did work, her small income was expected to contribute but it didn't buy her any decision-making power.

Brenda couldn't get anything right, no matter what she did—because of her husband's control and abuse. When Brenda spent more money than he liked, her husband distorted the situation to portray her as financially irresponsible. It didn't matter whether she bought groceries or something he asked her to pick up for him. Whatever she did, he spun a tale of woe to justify giving her an allowance. After she purchased window dressings—that he asked her to buy—he went on and on, putting her down and ridiculing her judgment.

Criticism in money matters, in time, became criticism about everything: mothering, keeping a home, even her physical appearance. Brenda felt beaten down, confused, and she doubted herself, which over time made her vulnerable to believing him.

Like Brenda's husband, controlling partners change your feelings, thoughts, and perceptions by:

- Exploiting small differences that exist between you

- Building on slight shifts in power

- Increasing his control in small increments with abuse tactics

- Making each abusive attack a bit more effective to ensure he gets control

Eventually, your positive beliefs in yourself diminish as your perceptions of your partner's influence and capability grow. In her book on brainwashing, Kathleen Taylor explains how this works. She says human brains are:

> … bad at detecting long-term, cumulative change if each step of that change is very small. From the start, the abuser may exploit this weakness by testing his partner's tolerance in small ways, perhaps with a snide remark here or there. A victim of abuse may initially register each individual put-down as trivial ("He's tired, he's had a bad day, he didn't mean it"), and unless she has made that special effort and conceptualized the remarks as part of a whole (as a concerted campaign, whether planned or not, by the abuser) she will not keep track of them—or their cumulative effect on her self-esteem. (Taylor 2004, 87)

In time, Brenda was coerced and persuaded to see her husband as the one who knew best about their joint money, and eventually about school for their children, weekend plans, extended family visits, and times with friends. Most tragically, she came to believe his negative perspective of her. It would be a decade later, during her divorce, that she would learn that he hid large sums of money from her in a separate bank account. In a number of ways, Brenda's marriage cost her dearly.

## As Your Partner Confines You, You Change

In intimate relationships, the heightened amount of time together impacts the couple and also each partner. In a healthy partnership, with care and support you grow as a couple and as individuals. With a controlling partner, you're not only unsupported, you become apprehensive. In time, you can be worn down by mistreatment and lose who you are—your identity.

Women in the recovery groups discover ways their partner—slowly and insidiously—created changes in their relationship that resulted in negative changes within themselves. And that is something I'd like you to reflect on.

Over time, as your partner changes, so do you. You may start out feeling confident, expressing your opinions and ideas freely. But his responses to you slowly become less accepting. Then he frequently expresses frustration with you. This grows more intense and intimidating. Since his love matters, you attempt to make changes to get a different reaction from him. Once you are met with the same hurtful responses repeatedly, you start holding back your thoughts and needs, maybe just a little at first. But you eventually stop trying to address concerns with him altogether because it's too painful. You just don't want to deal with the fallout—his rage, the put downs, the stress, and the hurt. You give in on little things to keep the peace, only to find yourself also accommodating his bigger decisions. You adjust to get along.

Brenda shared that "For a long time I forced myself to keep up appearances—what else could I do? I pretended to have a nice life with a successful husband and a beautiful home. I definitely needed to keep this up all the more when I became a mother. I just can't believe I was so trapped. I can honestly say that my marriage became the loneliest and scariest place to be. Even worse was living each day feeling so lost because I didn't know myself anymore."

To "get along" with a controlling partner, you're required to keep parts of yourself suppressed and hidden. In the end, by not speaking your thoughts or sharing your reactions to things, you gradually transform. While you're unaware of losing touch with yourself—what you need, want, and desire—over time, the impact of his abuse grows deeper and the wounding becomes more profound as you endure psychological harm and trauma. When you're slowly taken over by your partner's control and injured by his mistreatment, it's inevitable that you experience many significant losses that ultimately include important parts of yourself.

## Your Changes Are Losses

When I asked a group of women what they were like before they ever met their partners, one woman said, "I was definitely happier than I am now and very independent. I really miss that." Another woman chimed in to say, "Me too. I made all sorts of decisions for myself. Now I feel so confused I often can't make even the simplest choice." Two other women talked about how capable they felt prior to their relationships and how unsure they had become, how they came to feel less confident.

During her recovery, Brenda recognized how her husband slowly took over her life. She could see his abuse in the ways he tormented her and caused her to feel inferior while pumping himself up as superior. Although she tried, she couldn't get anything right because he intentionally distorted reality to make her out to be wrong—every time. As a result, she struggled with feeling worthless and stupid. Her recovery helped her to see how she came to believe and value her husband's perspective more than her own. In the end, she learned she had internalized his hurtful, false accusations into painful, negative beliefs about herself.

EXERCISE: What You Lost

Take a moment to see what changes have taken place inside you as a result of your experience with a controlling partner. As you just learned, psychological wounding is typical. To help you identify whether this is your experience, answer these six questions. As you answer each question, write down in your journal any specific or additional details that come to mind.

Use the following scale to rate how you feel about each statement.

1—Strongly disagree

2—Somewhat disagree

3—Feel neutral

4—Somewhat agree

5—Strongly agree

Record your responses to these statements:

- You felt better about yourself prior to knowing your partner.    5

- You went from being independent to gradually giving up what you like to do.    5

- While you once felt capable and trusted your judgment, you now feel unsure and experience self-doubt.    4

- You have lost confidence and self-esteem.    5

- You often feel anxious, scared, or depressed.    5

- While you once felt optimistic about your future together, you now feel discouraged as reality drifts further from what you had imagined your relationship would be.    5

Add your points to get your total score, which offers another piece of information about your experience with your partner.

If you scored less than 10, you're in good shape at the moment.

If you scored between 10 and 15, you're not experiencing many negative effects—yet.

If you scored between 15 and 20, you are being mildly impacted.

If you scored between 20 and 25, you are experiencing emotional effects that negatively impact your life.

If you scored between 25 and 30, the amount of stress you are under is making your day-to-day functioning difficult.

Your score reflects many changes and profound losses from the experience with your coercive partner. This recognition can feel unsettling, sad, and even heartbreaking. Whether you're dating or committed, take your feelings seriously—trust them. Your feelings are a response to seeing the many negative effects of your partner's behavior on you, which underscore your reasons to keep working on your recovery.

## Building Internal Resistance

Recovery involves becoming aware of new information and then using that information to change. The change that you're working on right now is *not* between you and your partner but inside you, a place where you have control or can develop it. You've been working on this change by coming out of denial, identifying your partner as controlling, and looking at how you came to be with your partner. In these ways, you have been deconstructing your experience and, ultimately, your entrapment. The more you know, the more you can use that knowledge to make changes for you.

You don't need to outwardly resist your partner since that could, in certain circumstances, cause you greater harm. Now, and throughout your time with this book, you will find that building internal resistance to your partner's coercive influence is the best way to get back in charge of yourself. From this place of strength, eventually you'll be in a much better position to address your concerns directly with your partner, if you choose to.

Recovery helps you regain what you lost, develop a stronger self, and come to trust your own judgment again. You are learning about your partner's coercive process, which can lead to brainwashing and changes in how you feel, think, and see things. As you grow through understanding the full depth of your partner's influence, you can address and reframe the negative beliefs about yourself that you developed as a result of his abuse.

One way to start rebuilding self-esteem is to revisit the negative beliefs you hold about yourself, deciding what is true and what is a distortion your partner made up to coerce you. In essence, this type of deprogramming frees you up to get back to yourself—what you feel and truly believe. As you do this, your confidence grows and the power of your partner's control decreases. In Stage Three, we'll address this in depth.

Brenda worked on her recovery, including her negative beliefs, until she was able to take back her life. This culminated in representing herself in court against her husband because she could no longer afford a lawyer. In every sense of the word, she had her day in court. She spoke up, made her case, and won. If the story of Brenda's successful recovery is helpful, let it be an inspiration to keep working on yourself.

## Check-In

It's difficult to pay attention to what you're learning with this book and also to what you begin to see with your partner, day to day. So I would like you to take a moment to check in with yourself. As I am sure you know, this process can be emotional: scary, anxiety-provoking, sad, and even depressing. Although these are all common reactions, they do make it hard to cope, so take care of yourself at the same time you're doing this work. A simple breathing practice can help. Breathing is calming and helps us to physically relax our bodies.

EXERCISE: Breathing into Calm

You can do this breathing exercise anywhere and for any length of time. When you're ready, take a number of slow, deep breaths. While breathing, stay focused on inhaling and then exhaling. When you breathe out, pay attention to the very end of your breath and then pause before your next inhalation. This break in your breathing is particularly beneficial (van der Kolk 2014). Do this breathing exercise regularly as well as in any moment when you notice that you're anxious or stressed.

Be sure to do things that make you feel better, whether it's some activity alone that always lifts your spirits, or time with people you enjoy. Make plans you're able to follow through with successfully, without your partner sabotaging them. Start a self-care routine of some kind. Prioritize self-care activities the best you can—you deserve it. Some suggestions for self-care include:

- Slow down and breathe

- Spend time with supportive people

- Take a walk, run, swim, or bike ride, or work out at a gym, as moving is always helpful

- Do yoga or gentle stretching

- Soak in a bath with music and candles

- Go to church, temple, mosque, or your place of worship

- Pursue a new hobby or activity you have been considering

## You've Got This!

Your controlling partner uses coercive tactics—slowly and insidiously—that gradually take over your life. This often becomes obvious in the commitment stage. In this chapter, you explored the hurtful impact of his coercion and the negative changes and losses they cause for you. At the same time, your recovery is not only possible, it is a path for gaining personal strength so that you can feel good about yourself. Next, we examine the powerful impact of the cycle of abuse.

CHAPTER 7

# Resist Falling into the Cycle of Abuse

In the last chapter, you learned that once you're beyond dating, your partner's control shows up—restricting your life in little and big ways. After a controlling relationship is established, these changes in your partner's behavior can form a pattern of abuse that can keep you trapped in a relationship, even for years. In this chapter, you'll learn about the abuse cycle and see how it works in your relationship. This insight will help lay the groundwork for you to see the powerful ways you're drawn back into denial making it, at times, harder to help and protect yourself.

## The Cycle of Abuse

Your partner's controlling tactics, while subtle at first, gradually grow more explicit and then, all of a sudden, they can seem to disappear completely. He becomes attentive and caring toward you. When he is by turns kind and hurtful, you might think that he's moody or that he has a Jekyll and Hyde personality with severe ups and downs. The truth is that your partner is acting out a cyclical pattern of abusive behavior, even when his behavior doesn't appear to be abusive.

A theory by Lenore Walker can help you look at how your partner's changing behavior may fit the cycle of abuse. Walker's cycle theory of violence (1980) addresses patterns of behavior that exist in abusive relationships, even when a partner is not physically violent, and shows that abuse is rarely constant. Rather, there are distinct changes during various phases in the cycle. The overall impact of the cycle is that it can allow a controlling partner to keep you initially engaged and eventually held captive week after week, month after month and, unless addressed, year after year.

When one woman shared that her physically abusive husband "can be the sweetest person," I responded: "Here lies your biggest obstacle to overcome."

## How You React to Your Partner's Abusive Behavior

Walker's cycle of abuse is based on an abusive partner's behavior during each phase of the cycle, but in this book the focus is on your experience. When the cycle of abuse is operating, you will experience different reactions within you; in other words, each part of the cycle elicits different emotional responses. With this in mind, I adapted Walker's work to reflect the customary responses and have labeled each phase according to what's typical to experience. This will help you become aware of your internal sensations and feelings at those particular times in the cycle. That way, you can focus more easily on your experience—not just on your partner's behavior. As your feelings become more familiar, you can know where you are in the cycle and what you can expect. Then you are better prepared to protect yourself.

We'll follow phases similar to the ones Walker identified. The following diagram illustrates the sequence of reactions and phases, with Walker's phases in parentheses.

- Reaction in Phase 1: Staying vigilant (as a result of partner's tension-building behavior)

- Reaction in Phase 2: Feeling trapped and terrified (as a result of partner's acute abuse)

- Reaction in Phase 3: Feeling hopeful for change (as a result of partner's reconciliation/honeymoon and calm period)

## Your Reactions to the Cycle of Abuse

Adapted from L. Walker's cycle of violence theory

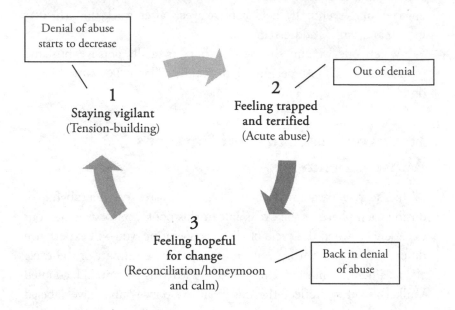

# Phase 1: Staying Vigilant (in the Midst of Tension-Building)

During Phase 1 of the cycle, you may detect some tension in your partner so that you feel you're walking on eggshells or in a minefield. He may slowly become more irritable, impatient, and critical. You're likely to react by exerting greater care to anticipate doing things right. You may not be fully aware of it, but you take on the mission to prevent "setting him off."

Like most women, you may believe that you can stop your partner's behavior from escalating into serious, intense abuse. This is because he has told you that you're to blame for his abusive outbursts. During this phase, you try to stay vigilant about what you say and do in order to keep him from becoming cruel and hurtful. At this point, while you may feel like you can control his outbursts, you ultimately have no control over your partner's behavior or abuse.

Jen's story demonstrates how this phase plays out. Jen is a sweet, youthful thirty-eight-year-old mother of three young children who took time off from a nursing career to be at home with them. Her husband, Rob, is a math teacher at their local high school.

Jen knew something was going on, as lately her husband had been tense and irritable. While she was standing at the kitchen sink clean-ing dishes, a sick feeling in the pit of her stomach returned. She felt exhausted from the day, but also from feeling tense about not knowing what to expect from Rob. As always, she tried to plan ahead. A little earlier she had picked up toys and settled her children in front of the television. From the other room, she heard only the sounds of Wilbur the pig talking with Charlotte the spider. Then the sound of driveway gravel crunching grabbed her attention. Jen felt her breath catch as her chest tightened. She told herself to keep breathing as she worried whether the house was neat enough, the kids quiet enough, and the dinner cooking in the oven good enough.

Do you ever feel like this? Do you try to stay a step ahead and on your partner's good side by accommodating his wishes in attempts to keep him from getting angry and attacking you or, for the sake of others like children, to keep him from escalating to a loud, raging outburst? From this state of vigilance, you might initially minimize the subtly increasing tension between you, but eventually your stress builds to a point you can't ignore anymore. Your partner becomes more openly irritated, obviously angry, intimidating—taking more control. No matter what you do or do not do, you cannot prevent your partner from increasing his hurtful attacks.

## What You Don't See

In your reaction during Phase 1, you may not see that:

- When your partner becomes tense, you minimize the problem that exists between you.

- You start changing your behavior to get him to change his behavior and reduce the tension.

- All along, you don't realize you're at risk of minimizing the potential danger ahead.

# Phase 2: Feeling Trapped and Terrified (in Response to Acute Abuse)

Eventually, your partner's behavior escalates to being unpredictable and highly abusive, inflicting psychological trauma on you (and young witnesses). The psychological abuse during this phase is quite serious and highly injurious to both your mental and physical health. He may shame and devalue you by targeting your areas of vulnerability—such as not feeling like a good mother or feeling guilty. You might feel terrified about the possibility that he could become violent. He might even hit, push, or beat you, which is physical abuse that puts you at serious risk for physical injury and, in some cases, even death. Feeling "trapped and terrified" by his painful, menacing attacks causes you to feel powerless, paralyzed, and traumatized. Safety planning can be put in place anytime—just jump ahead to chapter 10, "Threats and Physical and Sexual Violence."

Jen knew it was coming. Rob had been agitated for days after he learned about potential layoffs at work. He was prickly and frequently sent verbal barbs flying. She felt sick with stress as she stayed on high alert. All her attempts to help him to feel better or just calm down didn't work. Jen decided to go to the park with the kids before he returned home. Giving him some time alone at the house might be nice for him, she thought.

Her friend, Sara, invited Jen's three kids to stay a little longer at the park under her supervision, so Jen returned alone. She thought she would take advantage of the time to get dinner started. Just as she entered the kitchen, she heard loud footsteps. Her husband stormed into the room yelling, "Where the hell have you been? Where are the kids?" Moving away from him, she explained about the park, and thought how fortunate it was that the kids weren't around. He looked so agitated—red faced, veins bulging.

"You stupid fool—how would I know that?" He strutted over to her until his tall frame was a few inches away, wedging her between the counter and the table. As he stood over her, he raged on and on and she felt his spit hit her face as he called her vulgar names and told her just how pathetic she was—even as a mother.

Phase 2 is when he's highly abusive and traumatizing to you. You, and your partner, are not in denial during these kinds of episodes. You are deeply affected and can feel a great deal of emotional pain from the abuse.

### What You Don't See

In your reaction during Phase 2, you may not see that:

- The highly abusive incident puts you in grave danger.

- His extreme form of abuse is characteristic of his control and is what you need to keep in mind during the calmer phases of the cycle for it will come again.

- Children, as young witnesses, are at risk of being traumatized by watching or hearing the abuse.

## Phase 3: Feeling Hopeful About Change (in Response to Reconciliation/Honeymoon and Calm)

Phase 3 of the cycle is the aftermath that follows your partner's highly abusive behavior. After his angry explosion, your partner backs off and the tension between you diminishes or disappears completely. Many changes can then occur. Your partner can shift his behavior to something positive, intending to seduce you back. He may even revert back to that caring person you fell in love with in your courtship days. During this phase, your partner's favorable change—amplified with apologies and promises to change—can make you feel hopeful about the relationship going forward. At the same time, you are both in serious denial of the abuse that just happened. At this point, when you overlook the abuse you are keeping yourself in danger of further abuse.

Upon waking after a restless night of sleep, Jen's thoughts went immediately to the day before when she returned from the park. She could still see the horrible image of Rob's raging, red face. *Thank god*, she thinks, *Sara called to say she was on her way to the house with the kids*. Just then, loud shouting interrupted her thoughts: "Daddy!

Daddy!" Jen put on her robe and went downstairs to find out what was happening. As she approached the kitchen, she heard laughter. There, she saw her three children with their Dad making funny-face pancakes. Rob smiled at her and said, "We were going to surprise you with breakfast in bed."

Later in the day, when they were alone, Jen's husband told her, "I'm sorry." She heard how much he loves her and the explanation that it upset him to find everyone gone when he got home. If she had left a note, he would not have gotten so mad. Surely, she can see just how much they all mean to him. When he reached for her, Jen let herself be drawn into his familiar arms and while being gently kissed she heard a faint whisper: "It won't happen again."

Your partner may come around. He may apologize for his abuse, promise to change, or simply become more attentive again. He may arrive with gifts, flowers, initiate an evening out, or offer to watch the kids for you. Generally, he behaves more positively toward you. When the abuse was acute, you may have felt clearly how wrong, unfair, and outrageous his behavior was. But in the reconciliation period, with the favorable shift in his behavior, you may end up becoming ambivalent about what, exactly, occurred. This can lead to some rethinking on your part, especially if he convinces you that you were at fault in some way or it wasn't as bad as you're making it out to be. When he reassures you of his love, your commitment to him gets solidified and you go on with the relationship.

When Jen shared this painful episode in recovery, she recalled how difficult going through all three phases had been, and then added: "It all could have been avoided if I had just left a note." We can always disappoint and cause other people to be upset and angry with us. But each of us is responsible for how we choose to handle our feelings, including anger. If Jen had left her husband a note, yes, it would have given him the information he wanted. But the fact that she didn't in no way justified his outrageous tirade. Like other controlling partners, her husband had many other options, including expressing his feelings in a constructive way such as, "Jen, next time could you leave a note? I get upset when I don't know where you are with the kids." However, this type of communication is not a priority for someone like Rob who resorts to control.

In Phase 3 of the cycle, you're persuaded to overlook the abuse. If your partner implies he was made to behave the way he did because of something your said or did, you might see his point and feel a little guilty—maybe even taking on some of the responsibility, given the way he explains it. This is when you need to separate and sort out your behavior from your partner's distortion.

Does he assure you his bad behavior will never happen again, insist that he'll seek help if necessary (yet he never does), and convince you that he will change? Or, you might have a partner who suddenly appears to be in a better mood and goes on as if nothing happened. At this time in the cycle, both you and your partner are in grave denial about the abuse that took place. Open your eyes to see his behavior in the spirit in which it is intended: to get you to ignore his abuse and to seduce you back.

## What You Don't See

In your reaction during Phase 3, you may not see that:

- Your partner's blaming maneuver results in you feeling responsible for his abuse.

- You let go of the feelings of resistance to your partner that you had when he abused you.

- Your denial returns and overshadows the terrible abuse that just took place.

- You reconcile yourself to your partner and the relationship with renewed hope for a better future.

The positive change in your partner—the return of this familiarly nice person—can instill hope for lasting change. It may feel like, "He's back!"—the person you have loved, bonded with, and planned a future with. You start to think that maybe things can be better and feel happy that you can still have the wonderful relationship and family you always dreamed about. In the calm period, life continues but without—or mostly without—hurtful attacks. This may further your hopes for a lasting, better relationship. What you don't see is that this is an illusion created by your partner that doesn't hold up over time. The cycle never ends and the abuse continues.

A few weeks later, Jen's "loving" husband started in on her once again, this time over the shower. After a cold shower one morning, he got in her face, screaming about just how stupid and incompetent she was in taking care of the house. She thought, *How could I possibly know there is a problem with the hot water heater? It was fine yesterday.* But she knew to keep it to herself.

In the third phase of the cycle, the positive interchange with your partner instills hope for a better future that strongly fosters a desire in you to reconcile—to overlook the abuse and come back together. Each time puts you at risk of denying the abuse and being seduced back into the relationship, again and again. You remain in a confusing confinement with some moments of hope for a better future that reinforce your effort to somehow make it all work. Ironically, this wonderful, hopeful time is the most misleading and entrapping of all.

Penny shared that "I fall in love all over again when my husband becomes nice. It's truly a wonderful time, with us interacting around the house, laughing, and going out together. I always believed he had finally changed and that added to feeling good. But then, he shows up being irritable and begins to say things to me that hurt. I would once again feel devastated."

During the hopeful period, when their partners are nice and even caring, many women see this as an important time to get their needs met. One woman shared, "This was the time I could get money for our kids' sports programs. I had to plan ahead for these times." Upon learning about the cycle, another woman shared, "I was in Phase 1 and needed to be in Phase 3 by the next weekend. I incited an argument that led to his abuse (Phase 2), so he would be in a friendly mood when he joined my extended family and our children for a special event." In these small ways, women took advantage, perhaps in the only way they knew, to use the cycle they were stuck in to get basic things for themselves and their children.

Some women might look forward to this time of reprieve, not with hope anymore, but with some relief as the intensity of the abuse declines. The longer you cycle together, the more you learn that his turning "nice" is not so nice anymore. Maybe there are no more flowers or kind words, just an absence of abuse. When there's greater insurance you won't leave because you are too worn down by his longstanding abuse, your controlling partner doesn't need to seduce you back. He can even walk away after an abusive episode as if nothing happened. For some, you cycle between Phases 1 and 2 with Phase 1 now feeling like a reprieve.

In summary, the positive behavior that shows up in your controlling partner after an intensely abusive episode is a coercive tactic. (We'll revisit this coercive tactic, which is called "occasional indulgences" in chapter 11.) When you can see his caring behavior following his abuse for what it is—manipulation—you will create an important break in your entrapment. Without this insight, your partner's favorable behavior keeps instilling hope in you for a better future while he remains in control, and you stay psychologically captive. The constant repetition of the abuse cycle wears you down.

No matter how genuine he appears and no matter how hopeful you feel, eventually a controlling partner will let you down in these ways.

- Your partner will reveal his controlling nature once again—subtly at first, then overtly.

- You will find yourself back in Phase 1, walking in a minefield with mounting tension, prompting you to keep vigilant to avoid setting your partner off and to stay out of harm's way.

- Your partner will once again escalate and become highly abusive, entrapping and terrifying you.

- After the acute abuse ends, you will find yourself in Phase 3, the intermittent reprieve from abuse—with your partner professing his love, making promises, or at the least, not being intensely abusive for a period of time. Eventually, though, the cycle will begin again.

## Resisting Reconciliation

It's critical to recognize and understand that your partner's favorable behavior following his intense abuse is a manipulation to pull you back in so you reconcile. His coercion distorts your thinking, feelings, and perception. Only when you understand this can you get clear about what really is happening. Keep the following in mind.

- You know it is terrifying and wrong when he abuses you. Don't minimize or deny the abuse later. You need to hold on to this truth to protect yourself.

- You need to fight against the enticement of hope for change in Phase 3, no matter how good the promise feels. Stay grounded in reality: this is the same person who controls and abuses you. And none of the promises he's made before have come true, right?

- You need to sort out your partner's blaming accusations from your actual behavior and determine what is true for you. When you do, your partner's tactics will have less effect.

In the next exercise, you'll start building internal resistance to your partner's manipulation and blame by seeing exactly when you're entering the cycle of abuse, and which behaviors your partner is using to keep you there.

## Looking at Your Own Relationship

In this chapter, we have addressed the cycle of abuse and identified some broad, yet powerful, influences that show how controlling partners stay in control and confine you in the relationship. Recovery includes building internal resistance to your partner—by seeing his manipulations clearly, even the positive ones—to get out from under his hold.

Now it's time to look at your own relationship and reflect by considering some questions that will help increase your awareness. As you get clear about your experience, you will be in the best position to rescue yourself and you will also be far less likely to overlook key indicators in the future. This is because you will know exactly what his coercive tactics look like.

EXERCISE: Your Experience with the Cycle of Abuse

The abuse cycle plays out differently in different relationships and while it doesn't fit all controlling relationships, it does apply to many. The time it takes for you to go through a complete cycle can vary from one woman to the next. It may take hours, days, or months. During each phase, pay attention to your partner's behavior and your feelings in reaction to his behavior.

This is a journaling exercise. When you're settled and ready, begin. Identify your experience with each phase of the cycle. Then reflect on the "Recovery Tips" and write down any thoughts or insights that arise.

**Phase 1: Staying Vigilant**

- Are you on alert, feeling tense, walking on eggshells or in a minefield?

- Do you start altering your behavior with the hope to keep your partner from getting worse or escalating?

- What do you do?

*Recovery Tip*: Remember that you do not have control—he does—and you cannot change or prevent his abuse. You can only take steps to protect yourself.

**Phase 2: Feeling Trapped and Terrified**

- Does your partner's intense psychological abuse trap and terrify you?

- Are you fearful that his abuse will escalate to physical violence?

- Is he usually or always physically or sexually violent and you know you need to protect yourself but are not sure how? Turn to chapter 10 for safety planning.

*Recovery Tip*: Keep his intense abuse and your feelings about it in your consciousness the best you can, even when your partner relents and moves into Phase 3. This awareness helps you to take realistic steps to protect yourself going forward.

**Phase 3: Feeling Hopeful for Change**

- After an abusive episode, does your partner shift to apologies, caring behavior, or gifts?

- Does he convince you, or try to convince you, that he'll work on changing or that the abuse will never happen again?

- Does your partner convince you that it's your fault, that "You had it coming"?

- Does your partner play on your sympathy with threats of self-harm or suicide, or by bringing up his problems from a difficult childhood—all so you'll forgive him?

*Recovery Tip:* In Phase 3, stay aware of what's happening—your partner is coercively persuading you to deny to yourself how abusive and hurtful he was and can be.

As women in recovery groups learn about controlling partners, they start to pay attention to their experience in real time. You can do the same and look for "evidence" of control with your partner. After learning about the cycle of abuse, one woman reported, "I saw the cycle this week. I am definitely in that hopeful place." She saw the power of her partner's loving behavior, which in the past had always convinced her to overlook the prior abuse. But as she spoke those words, she was not in denial and felt extremely upset—and should be—given the way he had recently mistreated her.

## EXERCISE: Record Abuse for Reality Checks

To truly see your reality, you need to stay focused on the controlling, negative, or abusive behaviors. By documenting detailed descriptions of your partners' abusive episodes, with the dates when they occurred, during Phase 2, you will have a useful reality check to refer to. Just remember to keep your journal where it can't be found.

In the "nice" time, when you feel pulled back into the illusion of your relationship, you can read your journal entries to ground yourself in reality and recognize that his behavior is not genuine, that this is the individual who is also abusing you. You can also review the "Controlling Behavior Checklist" you completed in chapter 3. The goal is to stay out of denial by telling yourself the truth. Your partner is all of what these behaviors tell you about him—not just the familiar, caring behavior. Even though it can be painful, being able to regularly hold onto the fact that he's abusive will enable you to stay in reality and keep moving forward—out of captivity.

## Managing Your Response to Phase 2 Abuse

During Phase 2, you cannot go through a period of highly intensive abuse without being deeply affected emotionally, psychologically, and physically. Whether this period includes physical violence or not, you can become terrified and traumatized. Your body can hold the impact. Please take it very seriously. When we are threatened, we react with the impulse to fight, flight, or freeze.

- Fight is an impulse to anger or rage. To fight and react out of anger or rage can put you in greater danger with a controlling partner.

- Flight is an impulse to flee, to get away. But you don't have the freedom to easily leave, even to move to another room, when you're living with a controlling partner who can stalk you in your own home.

- Freeze is to implode—you become shut down, immobilized, and feel numb. You just don't feel. In my experience with women with controlling partners, this is your most likely reaction.

It's difficult to function well while you are in these reactive states. Attending to your reactions, when they occur, can lessen your response and help you cope. This would *not* be a time to journal about your negative feelings, instead you need to find ways to remove yourself from the emotional pain to get relief. Here are some tools to use when you're experiencing these painful periods. These can be used anytime you need them and no one has to know.

- When you feel a fight-or-flight response, your body becomes activated. Calming yourself is helpful. One way to calm yourself is to slow down and focus on your breathing. If you'd like, revisit the exercise in chapter 6, "Breathing into Calm."

- Another way to invoke calm is to describe your surroundings, identifying specific objects, colors, scents, and textures.

- Imagine or remember a safe and calming place such as a beach or favorite location and put yourself there. Focus on the various aspects of that place—what you see, hear, smell, and touch.

- If you feel a freeze response and you are shutting down, movement can help you get unstuck. Take a walk and be mindful of each step, jump up and down, throw a ball against a wall and catch it, play catch with your child. Or stand facing a wall, place your hands on the wall and push against it—doing this helps you to activate your muscles and body.

- In either state, yoga can be helpful because it integrates movement with breathing.

When we have experienced trauma in the past, our bodies are vulnerable to being triggered by something current that brings up the same unsettling feelings that may have occurred days, months, or years earlier. Your partner might say or do something that triggers in you a strong memory of a past event when he was highly abusive. He might also trigger trauma from another, earlier abusive experience that may have occurred as far back as your childhood. In that moment, you can feel and react as if you're reliving that old abusive episode. When this happens, it is important to remind yourself that this is old stuff that's coming up—you're not going through that experience in the moment. In the midst of a flashback like this, these grounding techniques can be useful.

- To reconnect with your self in the present moment, say or think repeatedly, "I'm here."

- Sit upright in a chair with your feet flat on the floor. Put your hands on the armrests and move them back and forth. Notice sensations such as feeling the texture on the arms of the chair, your feet solidly and firmly planted on the floor, and the way your body is anchored by the chair.

- Wherever you are, have a stone to grasp or something to smell that is soothing, like lavender from a vial of scented oil.

- Imagine a beam of sunlight shining into your body, from head to foot, that connects you to the earth. Tell yourself, "I'm here."

Experiencing and managing painful emotional reactions is not easy, but can be more bearable if you're not completely alone. Be sure to seek support and comfort when you can and in any way you can make it work, whether turning to a friend, family member, a therapist, clergy, or other resources available in your area.

Remember, as you keep working on your recovery, you're not only demonstrating courage, you are strengthening your ability to focus on your best interests and, in doing so, can eventually make changes in your life. Let's be sure to honor that as well.

## You've Got This!

In the commitment period, your partner's changing behaviors make up a cyclical pattern of abuse that puts you in positions with distinct reactions—each having a tremendous impact on you that contributes to feeling trapped. When your partner changes to more positive behavior and you feel, once again, the promise of a loving relationship, recognize this as an illusion he creates by manipulating you. This has the most captivating effect of all his attempts to control, but you can resist the power of the cycle by recognizing it for what it is.

CHAPTER 8

# See How Life Becomes
# "All About Him"

Take a moment to recognize what you're juggling. For you to look at
the depth of your experience with your partner, while being challenged
to see your partner's behavior as abusive, *and* cope with your feelings
and reactions as they arise is no small feat. Bravo!

The previous chapter showed us the cycle of abuse as a whole and
in this chapter we begin an in-depth look at specific behaviors that
drive it. For the next four chapters, I'll address a variety of coercive
tactics, identify their hidden injuries, and continue to offer you strategies for building internal and empowering resistance against a controlling partner's abuse.

## Controlling Tactics and Hidden Injuries

I've learned from women in recovery that it is very helpful for women
like yourself, with controlling partners who are trapped in a cycle of
abuse, to uncover just how you're taken captive psychologically.
Identifying both the coercive tactics your partner uses to forcefully
persuade you and the hidden injuries that these tactics inflict on your
psyche will help you deal with them. When clarity comes, you may feel
upset, but often women also feel relieved by what they didn't realize
and can now see.

Once you understand controlling tactics, you too will begin to see
your partners' tactics in real time—day to day. In your mind's eye (initially keeping it to yourself), you will label what you see as a specific,
coercive tactic at play. In the moment, this will help you to be grounded

and less vulnerable to the intensity of your partner's behavior. And as you're less impacted, the power of his tactic lessens. In this way, you develop internal resistance to your partner's control. At the same time, an important shift can take place—you feel some personal power. Your outward behavior toward your partner doesn't need to change until you are ready, but internally, with the new knowledge you have, you transform for the better. This is a huge step toward taking back control of your self.

## Psychological Abuse Embedded in Your Partner's Behavior

As I mentioned earlier, psychological abuse is very hard to see unless you know what to look for. Imagine that you are looking at your relationship through a large magnifying glass to perceive the specific coercive tactics that your partner is using. As we go through them, you will certainly come to see them very clearly. You'll see beyond what his behavior appears to be to what his behavior is intended to do—and does—to you.

Biderman's "Chart of Coercion" (Amnesty International 1973) is made up of the following eight coercive tactics—all having to do with psychological abuse.

- Isolation

- Monopolization of perception

- Devaluation and humiliation

- Demonstrating omnipotence or superiority

- Enforcing trivial demands

- Occasional indulgences

- Threats

- Induced debility and exhaustion

In this chapter, we'll address the first two coercive tactics: isolation and monopolization of perception. Chapters 9, 10, and 11 are devoted to the rest of the tactics. Along the way, you will see the multiple ways these tactics can play out in a relationship. You will have opportunities to identify and record your experiences. Not everyone experiences all the coercive tactics, or all the behaviors that can make up a coercive tactic. Just identify what fits your experience.

At the same time, keep the cycle of abuse in mind. Although all the tactics do not neatly coordinate with distinct phases of the cycle, some can. Whether an experience falls into Phase 2, acute abuse, or another phase has to do with the content and delivery of the abuse. But the most important determinant is what you experience through your reactions. Because it's not straightforward, I'll periodically make reference to the cycle so you can note where in the cycle the tactic you are experiencing is occurring.

## Controlling Tactic: Isolation

Isolation is a major coercive maneuver. Before we explore "how" a controlling partner isolates his spouse or girlfriend, I'd like for you to understand "why" they do. When you sustain connections with people other than your partner—even one other person—it can threaten your partner's power. Being connected with family and friends who care about you gives you access to support and, at times, opportunities to hear their concerns about your relationship. So your partner does not want you to hear that your loved ones worry about the way he treats you. These outside influences can undermine his control. He may also be jealous and possessive, wanting you all to himself. Once he reduces or even prevents social contact, you can become isolated. The more isolated you are, the more power and control he has over you—and that makes the other coercive tactics all the more effective to control you and your life. Mary, a twenty-eight-year-old wife, shared her story:

> My husband abandoned me within a month after we got married.
> I quickly learned that he had a double standard—he could do
> whatever he wanted but expected me to be home. He continued to
> see his buddies regularly after work. If I mentioned this, he became

*annoyed. He'd launch into lectures about how I always complained, I was never happy, and I was miserable to be around. He would say he needed a break from me and that's why he went out. If I went out with my girlfriends, he would be so suspicious and angry, implying I was unfaithful, that it wasn't worth the stress and heartache. Mostly, I was alone and in time I became very lonely.*

Mary has a story I have heard many times over the decades. As you read through all of the descriptions of isolation that follow, you will get a sense of the variety of ways it can be used as a tactic by a controlling partner. And it's likely you will see several of these isolating behaviors used by your own partner. Here are some other stories of isolation I've heard.

- He acts in ways that are humiliating to me in the presence of friends so I protect myself by not inviting people over.

- He ruins holidays by being excessively rude to my family and degrading to me in their presence. My family refuses to be around him.

- He's critical and insulting of family and friends when we're alone, so I stay away from them to avoid his wrath.

- He threatens to leave me if I stay connected with friends, or certain friends, so I have stopped seeing them.

- He decides who is allowed in the house.

- He ignores me at home by giving me the silent treatment. (This can go on for hours, days, weeks, and months—or in the case of one woman, two *years*.)

- He controls my time and takes away from any time for myself by forcefully expecting me to take care of the household, children, and his personal errands—from morning to night.

- He "doesn't allow" me to work, have interests, and do activities outside the home, actively discouraging them through intimidation.

- He intrudes on my workplace with frequent calls and visits, so that I end up at risk of losing my job. (Some women have, in fact, lost their jobs.)

- He demands to know what I am doing, where I am going, and who I am with—to the point that I forgo many things to avoid his harassing behavior.

- He looks at my cellphone, GPS, e-mails, he goes through my purse and briefcase—all in order to get information about my time away from him. (Women even discover spyware on their laptops.)

- He turns off my alarm or changes the time on the clock so I miss appointments or commitments outside the house.

- He controls the money, limiting my options to get something, go somewhere, or do something for myself. If I do spend money I'm required to show receipts, in part to reveal where and what I did while I was away from him.

- He has his friends watch me when he's not around. (One woman's husband was a police officer who, when he was on duty, arranged for others to surveil her and report back to him.)

As your partner devalues your friends, family, job, academic interests, and activities, you might gradually give them up to avoid the harassment and your partner's abuse. Then you have fewer to no other voices to counter what your abusive partner is saying and doing. These isolating tactics are hurtful and disempowering.

In addition to those profound losses, the isolation results in serious hidden injuries including increased dependency on your partner that gives him more power and influence over you, while you feel the slow deterioration of your spirit. With very little or no social contact, you become secluded and alone and, in the confinement, your reliance on your partner naturally grows. All the more, you look to the person controlling your life for what you need. In this place of isolation and dispirited state of mind, you feel less inclined to resist your partner.

# Looking at Your Own Relationship

Identifying whether, and to what extent, your partner is isolating you gives you information about how he achieves it. With this in mind, you can take steps, perhaps just one to start, to lessen your isolation.

## EXERCISE: Are You Isolated?

These questions will help you recognize your partner's isolating behaviors. As you read through each question, record in your journal how often you are on the receiving end of this behavior from your partner. Is it "rarely or never," "sometimes," "often," or "very often"?

- Do you feel you can't go out with friends or see your family when you'd like?

- Do you feel you can't pursue your own interests when they do not correspond with your partner's interests?

- Does your partner require you to tell him where you went or what you did?

- Does your partner call or text many times in the course of a day, dominating your attention so that you have little left for anyone or anything else?

- Does your partner restrict your access to money in a way that limits what you can do or who you can see?

Now, take a moment to look at your responses. If you mostly answered "often" or "very often," then your responses are telling you that you are being isolated, either some or most of the time.

It's important to understand the full depth of your isolation, so I'd like you to list other behaviors you experience from your partner that isolate you. Think about ways you feel alone and cut off from others, then look at whether they are the result of your partner's expectations, intimidations, and hurtful behavior. If it has been a while since you met with a dear friend, ask yourself whether it is because your partner made it too difficult to keep your friendship. Or perhaps you were working while you and your partner were dating, but he pressured you to leave your job before he'd agree to marry you. Your experience doesn't need to match any of the stories listed earlier—there are many more ways a partner can isolate you. Become aware of how your partner manipulates and coerces you into isolation. After you're done, try to consider orchestrating a way to decrease your isolation, whether it's connecting with another person, perhaps a friend you lost touch with, or some other way. You might be surprised how significant this can feel to your sense of well-being. Any movement out of isolation is a good start and you'll feel the benefits.

# Controlling Tactic: Monopolization of Perception

If by isolating you, by eliminating the "distractions" that take you away from him, your partner orchestrates the shrinking of your physical world, then with "monopolization of perception" your partner intrudes into your psychological world. You might have heard a more contemporary concept that's similar to this, known popularly as *gaslighting*.

With this tactic, your controlling partner declares reality for you and, if you have them, for your children. When I say "reality," I'm referring to the way your partner denies or distorts how things really are, in order to shore up his perception of how he sees things as the only one that counts. Here is what this tactic looks like.

- To keep the focus on himself—his needs, concerns, feelings, perceptions—he eliminates anything that competes for attention by invalidating, ignoring, discounting, or changing the subject.

- He declares that anything important to you—including your feelings and thoughts—are insignificant and wrong. Or if something doesn't reflect what he wants to hear, he refuses to listen.

- He withholds information, distorts the truth, lies, and claims that he never said or did something.

- He accuses you of distorting the facts and not remembering correctly—even when you do—and you can't convince him otherwise.

- He attacks your thoughts by questioning and scrutinizing, inferring that they don't make sense or are faulty—when they're not.

Women in recovery groups identify monopolization of perception as a central dynamic in their experience with controlling partners. Over time, they feel its profoundly debilitating effects as it causes confusion and self-doubt, leading to anxiety and depression. This undermines their ability to trust their own thinking and perception, making it harder to stand up for themselves. One woman in recovery, whose partner pressured her to give up her career, depicts the severe effects of being in a relationship with a psychologically abusive partner who distorted her reality to obtain control—all unbeknownst to her.

> I was a successful businesswoman, wife, and mother of two adorable children. We had a nice life in the suburbs. But over time I became consumed with self-doubt and started questioning my competence. When I began feeling exhausted and more confused, I felt I had no choice but to give up my prosperous business. I couldn't do it anymore. Even now, I can't explain to you what happened to me. I only know that I'm no longer the person I once was.

Let's look at how your partner might use monopolization of perception to gain control. As you read through the list of behaviors that characterize this, recognize the behaviors that speak to you. Let the examples help you get clear about how your partner manipulates you to instill self-doubt. Your partner may dominate your perception in any or all of the following ways.

- When conflict arises or the two of you disagree, he tells you with strong conviction that "You're wrong" or "You're stupid—you can't understand."

- He holds you responsible for his behavior by blaming you. Blaming accusations are all his deceptive twists and turns of reality that end up with you responsible for whatever goes wrong. It takes him off the hook every single time.

- He rewrites history. You bring up something he said at another time to discuss it and he denies saying it. He'll lie, distort, and manipulate to suit himself and stay in control. He might be the one to bring up the incident, but he changes a part of it and insists his account is the truth. He might appear indignant if you don't see it his way. You can't get him to admit the truth.

- When you decide to speak up about feeling bad in your relationship, your feelings are discounted. He claims, "You're too sensitive" or "You're overreacting." No matter how you approach him, you can't get him to listen to you or hear what you are saying.

- If he wants sex and you don't, he makes this out to be a problem of yours—he accuses you of being cold, frigid, or unloving.

- He distorts things you say to mean something negative. When you attempt to clarify what you said, he doesn't care and holds you to his distorted version—no matter what you say or even can prove. He uses it against you to agonize you.

- He needs to be right and in control, making you out to be wrong at all costs. One frustrated woman reported: "My husband said our child's temperature wasn't over 100 degrees, but it was 103 degrees. I know because I took it. He accused me of overreacting." Her husband was so bent on seeing his wife as wrong that he did so at the expense of their child's health.

- He makes false accusations such as, "You never listen to me," "You always think you're right," "You always have to have it your way," or "You're having an affair with your boss!" You can't convince him that these accusations are not true and he continues to torment you with his negative, degrading perception of you.

- He claims you are responsible for keeping him from being a better father. His children are less close to him than you and he accuses you of turning the children against him. He doesn't take responsibility for behaviors of his that may scare them and push them away.

- Mutual friends see his hurtful behavior toward you and withdraw from him. He accuses you of turning them against him.

- He decides you're "crazy" and accuses you of being crazy. But the truth is that living with coercive tactics—in particular monopolization of perception—can make you feel off balance, but you're not crazy. Your partner is trying to control the way you see the world so that you doubt yourself and back down. Then he can be right and in control.

## Monopolization of Perception Creates Self-Doubt

Your controlling partner constantly draws attention to his feelings and situations. He minimizes and denies your words or actions that are not mirroring back to him what he wants to hear and feel. If you're not yielding, he'll pressure you with words and intimidation until you are. This type of exchange, experienced over and over, causes confusion, anxiety, and self-doubt in you.

Using monopolization of perception tactics, your partner creates a very powerful brainwashing experience that causes you profound injuries. You may, like many women who arrive at the recovery groups, feel as if you are living in a fog. You may have lost confidence in your perceptions. Slowly, your partner eroded your trust in the way you see things and when this occurred, his position to dominate and control you strengthened. This is a very painful condition to endure and it makes you ever more vulnerable.

Almost the moment I met Jess, an accountant and mother of two girls, she blurted, "Please tell me if I'm crazy. I'm worried that I'm bona fide insane. For a long time, my husband has told me 'You're crazy!' and now I'm beginning to think he's right." She explained how she has been doing things and not remembering, like leaving her purse in one place and then going back to get it sometime later, only to discover that her purse wasn't there. Later, her husband told her he saw her leave it somewhere else. This same thing happened with car keys, the garage door opener, and other items. She found them somewhere other than where she remembered leaving them.

By the time she came for a mental health evaluation, these episodes of "forgetting" had been going on for quite a while. As it turned out, what Jess thought was evidence of her mind deteriorating was really her husband working to monopolize her perception to make her feel unbalanced. He would move objects, deny doing so, and cause her to feel confused and uncertain. Although it felt disconcerting to learn what her husband was doing to her, Jess mostly felt relief that she wasn't insane after all.

This "crazy-making" is also known as "gaslighting" after a 1938 stage play titled *Gas Light* in England and *Angel Street* in the United States. In the play, a husband convinces his wife that she is going insane because he claims she's imagining that the gas light in the house is dimming. But, all the while, he has indeed been dimming the light. Since the late 1990s, the term has been used to describe the sophisticated methods of manipulation that lead to loss of trust in one's own judgment. Its effects include a shift toward believing the controlling partner more than yourself, which results in him having more power over you in the relationship. To further illustrate, here is another scenario of how this works. Brianna, a fifty-year-old married woman, had been with her husband for ten years.

> When I met my husband, I had owned my business—a successful lovely bed-and-breakfast—for three years. After we got married, his attitude toward me, and my business, gradually changed but I did not see it then. He became disparaging about the ways I handled the business aspect of the inn, how I interacted over the phone with potential guests, and how I managed the hired help for cooking and cleaning. He was so confident in his perspective that often he left no room for my input. Little by little, I became more confused and uncertain about my ability to keep the inn going successfully. Eventually, with his urging, I sold it. It's only now that I recognize how he manipulated me.

Without trust in your own judgment and perception, it's almost impossible to act in your own best interest—as you will have lost sight of what that is. Your fallback position may be to accommodate him in order to get along, minimize the hurt, and survive. But in the end, it does not serve you well. Trusting your own judgment again is possible and an extremely important part of your recovery.

## Looking at Your Own Relationship

I know this can be a lot to realize and to sit with. You might have known your partner is "self-centered," hard to deal with, and actively controlling, but most likely you never understood the depth of harm his behavior has done to you. Remember: the more you know, the more you'll gain back trust in your own judgment and be in the best position to help yourself.

### EXERCISE: Is Your Partner Monopolizing Your Perception?

The following questions will help you examine the extent of your partner's monopolization of your perception. As you read through each question, record in your journal how often you are on the receiving end of this behavior from your partner. Is it "rarely or never," "sometimes," "often," or "very often"?

- Does your partner rewrite history, distort the truth, or deny things that you know to be true?

- Does he scrutinize your thoughts, making them out to be illogical or insignificant?

- Does your partner react negatively when you express or do something that's not consistent with what he expects?

- Does your partner make you feel you're wrong and to blame when things don't go well?

- Does your partner make accusations about you, deciding what you are and are not?

If you primarily responded "often" or "very often," you've identified that the monopolization of perception is playing out in your experience with your partner. The more you're aware of how this occurs,
the less confused you'll feel.

List the actual scenarios that illustrate your partner's behavior
when he dominates perception—when he manipulates your reality. For
help, go back to the questions and write down in your journal specific
examples of how he accomplishes each one. You might also note how
you felt at the time or how you feel now as you recall these scenarios.
Also, ask yourself whether his behavior fits a particular phase in the
cycle of abuse. As you see this tactic in real life, or recall more from the
past, add more examples to your list. It's a great reality check.

## Your Recovery: Building Resistance

This internal work will help you to trust your judgment, which is a
critical part of feeling stronger. I imagine that new feelings might be
emerging as you recognize what actually is taking place with your
partner. Women I've worked with often come to feel less confused
about what they're going through, validated in their experience with
their partners, and annoyed or angry with their partners for their
abusive ways. I imagine this may be true of your process as well. These
emotions are necessary for you to shift from self-blame to holding your
partner responsible. Use the annoyance, anger, or irritation—whatever
you'd like to call it—to propel yourself forward.

To resist manipulation, you need to have faith in your own perception. Recognize glimmers of your own awareness. Work on having and
keeping your own mental hold within yourself, even in those moments
when your partner is dominating and coercing. You can stand steady
with your new insight, knowing from within what is true for you. See
his behavior for what it is—label it as you come to know and understand what's happening. That will help you stay grounded in your own
perspective. In time, your self-doubt will be replaced with clarity in
your thinking and confidence in your own judgment. Eventually, you

will feel prepared to address what you feel, believe, and perceive is right for you.

## Check-In

Take a moment to see how you're feeling about what you learned in this chapter. Attending to your emotional safety helps to build your inner strength. As you need to, use the breathing exercise from chapter 6 or the coping techniques from chapter 7. If you need emotional support, reach out—in any way that you can do so safely—to a friend or someone you can confide in. At the same time, keep in mind the value of what you're learning and recognize the courage you have to do this work and to keep doing it. Take a break when you need to and do something that raises your spirits. Always attend to self-care the best you can and, if needed, revisit the suggestions in chapter 6.

## You've Got This!

Psychological abuse is made up of coercive tactics that include isolating you and monopolizing your perception—how you feel, think, and see the world. These tactics constitute brainwashing and inflict powerful hidden injuries on you, which underscores the seriousness of psychological abuse. You've begun to identify how these tactics play out in your relationship and that will help you get clear about the reality of your experience and be less vulnerable to your partner. These are all important goals you're working toward in your recovery.

# CHAPTER 9

# Take Back Your Strengths

You are moving right along. In the last chapter, you looked at two serious coercive tactics: isolation and monopolization of perception. We examined the hidden injuries caused by these two abusive strategies and identified what about them has been true in your experience. Although beneficial, this is hard work and you have kept up with it. You deserve to affirm yourself positively. Say or write in your journal: "Well done! I'm proud of myself."

We are continuing with Stage Two, when you continue to identify coercive tactics in your partner's behavior in order to deconstruct his hold over you. In this chapter, we will address three more coercive tactics, approaching them in a similar way. Keep in mind that these individual tactics may or may not apply to your relationship. The three coercive tactics addressed are:

- Devaluation and humiliation

- Demonstrating omnipotence or superiority

- Enforcing trivial demands

## Controlling Tactic: Devaluation and Humiliation

Devaluation and humiliation is a coercive tactic that controlling partners use to put you down and keep you "one down," at a psychological disadvantage. This powerful abuse tactic attacks your character and sense of self, creates immense shame, and damages your self-esteem. When you're ridiculed over and over by your intimate partner, you can internalize these hurtful accusations as negative beliefs about yourself—leading to a truly wounding experience. We feel badly about ourselves when we feel shame. The emotional pain is so great that in time you might attempt to sidestep this hurt at all cost. Women usually do what they can to avoid this profound psychological wounding, which becomes an ordinary response when you live with ongoing abuse.

## Devaluing Your Strengths

Over my years of doing recovery work with women, I have realized that put-downs and degrading comments from controlling partners tend not to be random attacks; rather, they specifically target the woman's strengths. The reason for this is that your strengths seriously threaten a controlling partner's power and control.

Lacey, a woman in her late thirties, reported, "I remember learning in high school that I am gifted intellectually. This has always been important to my self-esteem. Lately, I have felt so stupid and incompetent that I gave up my law practice." Lacey's husband is an example of how, by targeting a strength, an abusive partner can emotionally wear you down to the point where you lose an important part of yourself. During her recovery, Lacey shared that on a daily basis, usually during dinner, her husband excessively questioned, interrogated, and devalued her thoughts and ideas. In time, she came to feel more self-doubt; she no longer felt confident and did not trust her own judgment. In the end, she felt she couldn't continue to do her job well as a lawyer. Sadly, she gave up the one thing she said she truly enjoyed.

For some women, the fact that their partner feels threatened by their strengths made the abuse obvious, like it was for Julianne. She shared that her husband excessively criticized her about the way she managed the family budget and claimed he had to take over all the finances because she was so inadequate. Julianne was a successful accountant with a thriving practice, so it was clear her competence in the realm of finances threatened his control.

## How He Does It

In the list that follows, see if you share any of these experiences of being devalued and humiliated by your partner. For the most common behaviors, I have offered examples reported by women in recovery. Pay close attention to the anecdotes that resonate with your experience and, if you'd like, note them in your journal.

**He puts down your strengths and good intentions—you're never good enough.**

*Example:* Kendra loved to give dinner parties and she knew from feedback that she was very good at it. As she prepared, her husband would spend days harassing and criticizing her and acting more aggressive. Kendra said she couldn't bear it and stopped entertaining altogether. By the time she came to a recovery group, twenty years had passed since her last dinner party.

**He targets your vulnerabilities to shame you. If you're prone to feeling guilty, he'll find ways to make you feel guilty. If you have fears, he'll use them to make you feel afraid.**

*Example:* "You're like your mother!" Lily dreads hearing her husband shout this at her. She grew up with a mother who had mental health issues and early on she shared this painful history with her husband. Lily works hard to not be like her mother. Intellectually, she knows she isn't like her, but emotionally she is still vulnerable and her husband knows it. When he attacks her in this way, she becomes immobilized with shame.

**He humiliates you in public.**

*Example:* Carolyn's boyfriend makes her the focus of conversation when they're out socially by telling stories to humiliate her and be "funny" at her expense. He distorts her behavior, in a devaluing way, to shame her. When Carolyn attempts to talk about it later, he accuses her of being too sensitive.

**He humiliates and shames you when you're alone by bringing in the outside world.**

*Example:* "Everyone knows how pathetic you are." "All our friends think you're stupid, but you don't even see it." Charlene was more apt to believe her husband when he said things like this because she had difficulty trusting her own perception. When he focused on being "stupid"—an insecurity from childhood—coupled with being isolated, she felt incapable of checking out his accusations with friends.

**His accusations, although they are false, can feel deeply humiliating.**

*Example:* Maggie's husband accused her of affairs and insisted on checking her clothes and body for signs. Although the accusations were not true, she knew that if she refused he would take it as testimony to her guilt. So she went along with the searches and endured extreme shame and humiliation because of them.

**He coerces you to do something you know is wrong.**

*Example:* Ava ended up signing jointly filed 1040 tax forms even though she knew the information was inaccurate. She felt guilty and ashamed, but too fearful not to comply.

Here are some additional methods.

- He calls you names like "bitch," "cunt," "stupid," or "crazy," or says things like "You're a piece of shit." When this happens in front of children it can feel all the more devaluing and painful.

- He puts down, criticizes, and shames you about your role as a mother.

- He humiliates you by using sex to hurt and control you.

- He puts you down as a woman and puts down women in general.

- He criticizes you about your weight and devalues your body and appearance.

- He comments on other women's looks and sexual attractiveness to make you feel uncomfortable or badly about yourself.

## Decreased Self-Esteem

Being the recipient of devaluing and humiliating accusations and behaviors can deeply wound your sense of self—who you are. Devaluing and humiliating attacks are meant to make you feel shame, whether they focus on your character or undermine your strengths. The results are that you lose self-esteem—the ways you feel good about you—and feel powerless, which is a controlling partner's desire. In time, risking more attacks to your character becomes much more painful than giving in, so you choose to go along with him. When this involves going against your own standards, you can feel even more ashamed. It's a harmful cycle that can hurt and traumatize you.

I am deeply moved and saddened to think about the shaming experiences that some women go through. I can imagine you might be feeling similarly as you identify the ways your partner hurts you. Right now, your feelings validate the pain you endure. It's important to have some compassion for yourself. You do not deserve to be degraded or humiliated in any way.

## Looking at Your Own Relationship

Now we come to examining the experience with your controlling partner to determine to what degree he devalues and humiliates you to sustain power and control.

### EXERCISE: Does Your Partner Devalue and Humiliate You?

As you read through each question, recognize how often you are on the receiving end of this behavior from your partner. Is it "rarely or never," "sometimes," "often," or "very often"?

- Does your partner call you degrading names?

- Does your partner put you down by criticizing your looks, thoughts, or feelings?

- Does your partner attack your strengths?

- Does your partner attack aspects of you, including physical traits, that cause you shame?

- Does your partner humiliate you in front of others, in public?

- Does your partner devalue you to your children or in front of your children?

If you mainly responded with "often" or "very often," you're recognizing that your partner devalues and humiliates you.

Next, take out your journal and document his specific behaviors and your feelings. Compare how you felt about yourself before the relationship started and how you feel about yourself now. Looking at what he chooses to target in you can help you become aware of his devaluing and humiliating attacks. Identify the strengths, if so, that he focuses on and how you now experience these strengths within you. In addition, note when your partner uses this tactic and whether it is during a particular phase of the cycle of abuse.

EXERCISE: Impact of Being Devalued and Humiliated

Let's now look at the hidden injuries inflicted by devaluation and humiliation tactics. Use the following point scale to rate how you feel about five statements.

1—Strongly disagree

2—Somewhat disagree

3—Feel neutral

4—Somewhat agree

5—Strongly agree

Record your responses to these statements:

- My self-esteem has gone down during my relationship.

- I feel badly about myself.

- I give in to my partner to prevent him from degrading me.

- My partner uses sex to make me feel ashamed.

- I have gone along with my partner even when it's against my values to avoid painful attacks.

To score your responses, add your points.

If you scored 15 or lower, you don't have much to be concerned about.

If you scored between 16 and 20, you don't have the self-esteem to stand up for yourself.

If you scored more than 20, you're in great pain from the shame.

In recovery, you have an opportunity to feel better by taking back your strengths and regain positive feelings about yourself.

## Controlling Tactic: Demonstrating Omnipotence or Superiority

Many controlling partners believe they are superior and that, because they are *male*, they are entitled to power in the world. They might use their male gender to justify their use of the fear or intimidation that can make you believe that you and the family must behave subordinately—or else. Emily, a forty-three-year-old married woman, shared her personal experience with this.

*After we were engaged, we decided to purchase a house together. While we were looking I noticed that he was less open to my input—what I said I liked and didn't like. He had this way of making his preferences seem better—more reasonable—while implying mine were silly. But in the end, we had a wonderful home to move into and I was happy with the decision. However, before too long, he claimed it was "his" house and started making all the decisions about it. Eventually he made other decisions, too, insisting that "This is the way it is!" I came to feel inadequate and powerless to make a difference in our lives.*

The following examples from women in recovery illustrate how a controlling partner's belief in being superior drives his behavior—and keeps you one down. As you read through this list, pay attention to what feels or looks familiar to you. Again, you'll have an opportunity to explore your experiences in the next section.

- "He believes he can do what he wants and doesn't need to take others into consideration—ever."

- "He says, 'I'll do it my way, in my time!' He runs things—I have no say—life is on his schedule. As I get the children and myself ready to go somewhere, he pressures me to hurry up. Once we are all in the car, he's in the house making us wait— sometimes for half an hour. He's not accountable."

- "He makes all the big decisions—without my input—because he believes he knows best and is in charge."

- "Nobody tells him what to do—I have to do what he says. With my husband driving, we would all leave the house together in the van for a family outing. He would either not tell me where we were going, or tell me a place but it was never the truth. My solution was to have a few different tote bags ready in the car, so I could grab the one I needed. It is one way he keeps me off balance."

- "He defines my role as a woman, expecting me to be subservient."

- "I'm expected to look good because it reflects on him. He picks out what I wear."

- "He never apologizes because he believes he doesn't need to."

- "I need to guess what he wants, to read his mind, or to know he changed his mind and what he changed it to."

- "If I decide to speak up, he punishes me—there's always payback. Once in a while, I'd speak up about something I felt strongly about that he didn't like to hear. It was inevitable that I would pay the price. Perhaps not immediately, but in a day or two, I would be given a hard time and be intensely harassed and degraded."

- "He's entitled to give me an allowance, he makes me ask for money, he lies and withholds information about the family finances."

## The Superiority in Economic Coercion

Between 94 and 99 percent of women who experience domestic violence also encounter economic abuse (Postmus et al. 2012). Economic coercion is powerful, extremely damaging, and a subset of a belief in male superiority. Money is critical to the quality of our lives in so many ways. It also gives women choices and opportunities that controlling partners can find threatening. The results are that women with controlling partners can be:

- Prevented from getting jobs, or keeping jobs, if their partner does not support it

- Forced via threats and abuse to give their paycheck to their partner, obtain loans, or conduct other transactions to get money for their partner

- Have their names used to obtain personal loans or apply for credit cards without their knowledge

- Excluded from having their name included on the deed to the house, title to the car, or other joint assets

- Actively kept from any financial information

Without access to money, women who are mothers have difficulty caring for their children adequately, can become more isolated, and overall have a harder time getting by. Without money and resources, women are often more fearful to take steps to leave the relationship because they don't believe they can survive. In one group, a woman said, "I feel like I'm living in the 1950s when men were expected to work and be breadwinners and women were expected to stay at home caring for children, the household, and their spouse."

In addition to believing his male superiority entitles him to power and money, the controlling partner can feel entitled to sex with his partner. He makes the decisions about having sex—when, where, and how. I'll discuss this further in the next chapter under sexual coercion and violence.

Our culture often places men in positions of power. Not all men use this positioning against their partner. Controlling partners can, however, do so to justify and attain power over a girlfriend or spouse. It becomes one of the many ways a controlling partner coerces and brainwashes you to their way of thinking, causing great harm.

## Controlling Tactic: Enforcing Trivial Demands

If your partner believes he is superior because he is male and demands you remain inferior and subservient, you become far less important than him in the relationship. He can express this by setting petty rules and seeing to it that they are followed—if not, the rule violation gives him another arena to exercise his power by punishing. This describes another type of coercive tactic: enforcing trivial demands.

This tactic reinforces a practice of compliance that is disempowering. He decides for you and the family what needs to be done and how things should be done. You're expected to follow his demands or rules, but he doesn't follow through on what he is asking of you himself—he has a double standard. If you don't comply, he can employ enforcement by using excessive punishment. With his trivial demands, and serious threat of enforcement that can include violence, you become fearful, worn down, and more compliant as you stay vigilant in what you need to do.

Ultimately, you become vulnerable to threats of your partner punishing you or even abandoning you if you don't stay in "your place." Your desire to stand up for yourself dwindles and you can end up believing it's futile to resist.

# Looking at Your Own Relationship

Like other tactics, claiming superiority and enforcing trivial demands can create a sense of powerlessness—a debilitating emotional state. The work you're doing to help yourself, on the other hand, leads you to feeling more empowered. This is the best way to overcome powerlessness. Remember that as you turn to examine your own experience.

EXERCISE: Claiming Superiority to Keep You Inferior

Now is the time to examine your partner's behavior for ways he might use his belief of superiority against you. The following questions are about your partner's claim to be superior and omnipotent, although that doesn't mean they are true. As you read through each question, record how often you feel this way. Is it "rarely or never," "sometimes," "often," or "very often"?

- Does your partner believe he's entitled to be in charge?

- Does your partner make most of the major decisions, including those about money, without taking you into consideration?

- Does your partner expect you to be subservient and chiefly responsible for domestic responsibilities and childrearing?

- Does your partner never apologize or believe he doesn't have to apologize?

- Do you experience payback from him if you speak up or behave outside of his expectations?

If your responses are primarily "often" or "very often," your partner strongly believes he's superior to you and behaves that way. His expectation is that you act in a way that shows you're compliant or inferior to him—failing to do this can lead to some kind of hurtful reprisal.

## EXERCISE: Impact of Claiming Superiority

Let's look at how you might be impacted by being in a relationship with someone who claims to be superior to you. Respond to the statements that follow by selecting the best response for yourself using this point scale.

1—Strongly disagree

2—Somewhat disagree

3—Feel neutral

4—Somewhat agree

5—Strongly agree

Record your responses to these statements:

- I often feel that I'm damned if I do and damned if I don't—I can never get it right.

- I fear some kind of retribution if I do what I want, not what he expects of me.

- I'm scared he'll abandon me if I don't do what he wants.

- It feels futile or dangerous for me to resist him.

- I never get an apology.

To score your responses, add your points.

If you scored more than 15 points, you are experiencing some tension in this arena that would be worthy to recognize.

If you scored more than 20 points, it's clear you're dealing with a partner who wants you to believe you're inferior to him.

Try to appreciate what you are learning and understanding about your partner. You are not inferior, but you may assume such a role to survive and get along in the relationship—at least for now. This is an important distinction.

## Your Recovery: Build Resistance Within Yourself

Examining the three powerful tactics in this chapter can be eye-opening, scary, and leave you feeling more uncertain about your partner—even about being with your partner. If you're someone who has blamed yourself for the abuse you endure, I hope the self-blame is lessening as you come to understand your personal experience with your partner's controlling behavior. Although I have said this before, it needs repeating—you cannot make someone put you down and mistreat you.

As women in recovery talk about the ways they feel devalued, humiliated, and made to act inferior, they also reveal how they learned to protect themselves. After they realized that good and happy feelings would never be well received, they kept these feelings to themselves. If they had a good experience or got favorable feedback from a boss or coworker, they would choose not to share it with their partner. For they discovered that a controlling partner never shows he can be happy for you and that you deserve good things. Rather, he perceives your accomplishments as taking away from him. He's more likely to react by minimizing or distorting your positive skill or feedback to devalue you. It's likely that you already keep good things to yourself or only share with others who you know can be happy for you.

EXERCISE: Your Reactions to Your Partner's Abuse

As your self-blame lessens, other feelings might be emerging such as discontent, irritation, anger, or frustration with how your partner abuses you—and takes *no* responsibility. Recognize, feel, and take these emotions seriously. Allow yourself to sit with them. Journal about these emerging feelings and the shift from self-blame—even if you haven't fully turned this corner, the journaling may spur you on. If you can, talk to a trusted friend or individual so that you are not alone with your feelings and so they can validate you.

After you do that, there is one more step you can take as part of this exercise. Think back to an earlier time, perhaps before your relationship, and identify a strength that you remember about yourself. Once you fully recognize the strength, write about it in your journal and include the positive feelings that come up while recalling it. Do this for other lost strengths as well.

Then focus on how you lost touch with these strengths during your relationship. Recognize the devaluing attacks used by your partner that chipped away at this strong part of you. Journal about it. Think of Lacey—she never lost her gifted intelligence, she lost confidence and belief in herself. You too can take back your strengths and own them. Let them be wonderful parts of you again.

## You've Got This!

Controlling partners devalue and humiliate, often targeting your strengths—which are perceived as threats to their power and control. Some partners use "male superiority" to justify their position of power over you, expecting you to stay in an inferior role. Recognizing and reclaiming your strengths helps you to get back to your self, a stronger self, as you work on your recovery.

Next we look at threats and physical and sexual violence. If you're thinking this doesn't apply to you, I encourage you to take the time to read through the chapter to know for sure. Sometimes women want to skip the physical abuse or violence material, believing it doesn't pertain to their case—but then discover that it does in a way they had not known.

# CHAPTER 10

# Threats and Physical
# and Sexual Violence

Your commitment to continue your recovery is significant because it holds a growing commitment to yourself. This is what gets lost with a controlling partner and this is what gets found in recovery. I hope you're beginning to see the undeniable importance of prioritizing yourself to take back control of you.

As you continue to recognize the coercive tactics of controlling partners and the hidden injuries they inflict, I hope you take them seriously for the harm they cause and the ways they make you feel emotionally insecure. In this chapter, we continue to look at psychological abuse as we turn to another tactic: the use of threats. We start with general threats, then move to specific threats of physical harm that make you feel unsafe. Then we'll move to physical and sexual abuse/violence that, at times, results from a threat being carried out. This brings us to the aspect of domestic violence in which threats of harm and violence, both physical and sexual, have legal repercussions and options for legal protection. Domestic violence, also described as intimate partner violence, is defined by the US Department of Justice (2015) as:

> A pattern of abusive behavior in any relationship that is used by one partner to gain or maintain power and control over another intimate partner. Domestic violence can be physical, sexual, emotional, economic, or psychological actions or threats of actions that influence another person. This includes any behaviors that intimidate, manipulate, humiliate, isolate,

frighten, terrorize, coerce, threaten, blame, hurt, injure, or wound someone.

Intimate partner violence includes physical and sexual violence and psychological abuse. Threats to intimidate and cause harm to another fall well within this definition.

## Controlling Tactic: Threats to Intimidate and Harm

Controlling partners can use threats of all kinds to overpower their spouses or girlfriends to get them to do what they want. Threats are powerful, intimidating, and can stop you in your tracks and cause you to change your behavior in an instant to protect yourself. Threats are used to coerce, and controlling partners find out what works on you. Here are examples of threats that impact your life brought forth by women in recovery. As you look over this list, see if you recognize anything that describes your own experience.

- He threatens to abandon you if you continue with school, work, or seeing your family and friends.

- He threatens to tell untruths to hurt your reputation within your neighborhood, social circle, professional network, or religious community.

- He threatens to give you less money or no money and to take away or close down your credit card.

- He threatens to turn off service for your cell phone or computer.

- He threatens to report you as an abusive mother, with made-up accusations, to social services or others.

- He threatens to divorce you and take the children away by getting full custody. (Many women have reported that this threat is the most terrifying. It's only when they seek legal advice that they learn it's an unfounded threat.)

These non-physical threats impact your life in pervasive ways. They are one kind of threat. Another type of threat feels or sounds violent. They are implicit, yet intended to intimidate and frighten you. At times, you might feel a threat to your physical being just from your partner's intimidating demeanor, harsh words, angry gestures, or violent acts taking place near you. The impact is profoundly threatening to your safety and sense of well-being emotionally, psychologically, and physically—even though physically you are not touched. These violent acts are threats you need to take seriously. Let's look at what women in recovery groups identified. Again, pay attention when a description relates to your experience.

- He threatens to kill himself if you ever leave him.

- He gives you a menacing look to scare, intimidate, and threaten. The message is, "Watch out, my anger can escalate and get far worse." This is especially effective when he's been physically violent in the past so that the *look* is all that is needed to remind you.

- He uses the size of his body to intimidate you by standing too close and towering over you.

- He points a finger or shakes his fist in your face.

- He yells, screams, and has a temper tantrum.

- He threatens with words: "You need a smack upside the head," "You need to be taught a lesson," or "You know what's coming if you don't shut up!"

- He corners you or blocks your exit from a room.

- He threatens to hurt the children if you leave him, get a job, or defy him in some way.

- He threatens to kill you—murder you. It's serious and you know he's not just blowing off steam. You might start to fear times when you are vulnerable, like when you are asleep.

- He threatens to have you killed if you leave him.

- He threatens violence toward people important to you, like parents, siblings, relatives, or friends. You might cut off contact with those people in order to protect them or might not go to them in an hour of need because it could put them at risk.

- He drives recklessly in a way that feels threatening and scares you.

- He shows you weapons or keeps weapons around the house that frighten you.

- He threatens to hurt or take away your pet. He beats your pet in front of you.

- He threatens to harm you: "I'll make you regret saying that."

- He stalks you in your home and won't let you have privacy.

- He doesn't allow you to disengage from an argument or intense situation by leaving the room—he follows you.

- He stalks you outside your home. This can happen whether you're dating, living together, married, broken up, separated, or divorced. He follows you or lies in wait, shows up at work or an activity, or calls or texts incessantly to find out where you are and what you're doing.

## Impact of Threats

As you can see, threats of physical harm—whether your partner acts in an intimidating manner or directly threatens violence—are extremely scary and debilitating. Threats are meant to coerce and to create fear and anxiety. These threats are made more powerful when there is a history of physical abuse. To protect yourself, you're likely to do whatever you believe will minimize the possibility of your partner acting on his threats. This is an important way you take care of yourself and possibly your children. Having threats hanging over you, with the possibility of them transpiring at any time, is a powerful coercion tactic that can feel devastating and lead to despair through a loss of hope that your situation can change. In this moment, by reading this book and learning more, you're bringing back hope as you work on your recovery.

## Looking at Your Own Relationship

In time, threats can become so familiar that you no longer notice each time he threatens you. Take this time now to recognize the threats you live with.

EXERCISE: How Are You Threatened?

For this journaling exercise, find a quiet place to sit and reflect. Take a few minutes to settle into yourself. When ready, bring your attention to the experience with your partner. Identify whether or not he uses threats against you. If so, in your journal, make a list of the threats you receive.

As you do this, first think about threats you experience that would restrict your life in a major way if carried out. Then think about threats that feel or sound violent that intimidate you and impact your physical safety. Be aware of the feelings that come up and note them. If you can recall the dates when physically threatening episodes took place, write them down.

Going forward, as you remember threats, or when these threats occur in real time, add to your list. This documentation may help you obtain legal protection if and when you choose. I'll say more about legal protection in Stage Three.

## Physical Violence Takes Many Forms

When a partner is violent near or around you, doing things like punching a hole in the wall, the message is "Next time, this could be your head." In that moment, you are the witness and his violent episode is meant to intimidate and frighten you. Don't mistake his behavior as not intended for you; he is sending you a message. You don't discover signs of physical violence that have occurred in your absence, right?

Keep in mind that during physical (and sexual) violence, you are in Phase 2—trapped and terrified—in the cycle of abuse. Women from recovery groups report ways that their partners acted violently *near* them.

- Punches the wall: Just inches from Penny's head, his fist went through the bedroom wall.

- Breaks down a door: Melanie locked herself in the bathroom to get away from her husband and then watched, terrified, as he broke down the door.

- Kicks in a cabinet: Beth's movement to get away from her husband stopped when he put his foot through the cabinet.

- Throws objects: Gail's husband threw a ceramic figure that broke close to where she was standing.

- Throws a plate of food at the wall: After being told her dinner was "crap," Corrina sat stunned as he picked up his dinner plate and threw it against the dining room wall.

- Rips the phone out of the wall: Jenny watches while on the phone with her mother, who he claims to hate.

- Beats the dog or kicks the cat: Pam could only sit by in a frozen, traumatized state when her husband attacked their family pet.

- Destroys your meaningful possessions and things you hold dear such as, pictures, family heirlooms, or keepsakes: Marcie protected herself by never disclosing what she held valuable.

- Smashes and destroys furniture: Wendy's husband threw the coffee table through the picture window as she stared in disbelief and was terrified that she was next.

- Shows you weapons to scare you: Samantha found an illegal switchblade knife appearing on her bedside table periodically.

Physical violence that takes place near you can lead to acts of physical violence directed at you. But a physical attack—with the potential to harm, injure, disable, or cause death—can also occur without any preamble. Like psychological abuse, the purpose of physical violence is to gain power and control over an intimate partner. As I mentioned earlier, unlike psychological abuse, physical violence is the part of domestic violence that's recognized as criminal and against the laws we have in place. As a result, it has been examined, researched, and measured, which is reflected in these daunting statistics.

- Nearly one in four women in the US have been the victim of some type of severe physical violence by a current or past spouse or boyfriend during her lifetime (Breiding et al. 2014).

- When a gun is in a home where domestic violence occurs, the woman living there increases her risk of homicide by 500 percent (Campbell et al. 2003).

- 4 to 8 percent of women experience domestic violence while pregnant, with devastating effects to the mother and unborn child (Gazmararian et al. 2000).

Clearly, physical abuse and violence is serious and needs to be seen that way. It's not a moment of frustration or anger that got out of hand or an isolated incident, rather it is a choice that's made. Physically violent acts can include punching, kicking, shoving, slapping, shaking, pinching, hair-pulling, and restraining. The following list is gathered from the experiences of women in recovery and they may or may not have occurred in your relationship. Here are ways a partner may directly physically abuse you.

- Shoves you down the stairs

- Spits on you

- Drags you

- Rips off your clothing

- Painfully and excessively pokes at you

- Ties you up

- Throws objects at you

- Tries to run you over with his car

- Burns you

- Uses a weapon, such as a gun or knife, to harm you

- Tries to kill you

- Kills someone you love

- Chokes or strangles you

In particular, choking is a tactic of control all too common in domestic violence cases. Research shows that if your intimate partner chokes or strangles you, you are at a higher risk for injury and homicide than someone in a relationship with an abusive partner who has never been choked or strangled.

To illustrate, I'll offer some statistics from New York. In 2009, of all the women who died in the state as the result of an abusive partner, choking was the single largest violent act that occurred as part of their murder (Gulley 2011). In 2011, the state of New York made choking a crime, which resulted in two thousand domestic violence arrests within fifteen weeks.

Sadly, the women who have come through my recovery groups who reported being choked at some point did not always take it seriously. One woman named Helen made an initial attempt by showing a picture of the red marks on her neck to her husband, hoping he'd take his harmful attack seriously. He claimed she did it to herself, which is an example of monopolization of perception in which he lied and twisted the truth. Although physical abuse is criminal, controlling partners are apt to deny and lie about their abuse, but do not let that deter you from taking it seriously. In the end, Helen sought help outside her marriage.

## Escalating Attacks

With a controlling partner, physical violence is always a possibility. Luanne is twenty-nine and had been with her husband for more than a year before experiencing any physical abuse. During her recovery group, she shared this story.

*In the morning following an evening with our friends, I was telling my husband that I didn't like the way he belittled me in front of them* [which is an example of the coercive tactic of devaluation and humiliation]. *He instantly became angry and yelled, "You better watch what you say!" Then he pushed me. I was shocked. He had never touched me before. After that, I worried constantly when he got upset or angry that he could escalate and become physical again.*

This fear of escalation, in and of itself, is powerful and common when you're in a controlling or abusive relationship. Just knowing from experience with your partner that the abuse or attacks could escalate and get far worse is an enormous ongoing threat. Many women work to manage or even stop such an escalation. The ways you accommodate or comply—such as giving in, covering up for him, stating you didn't say or mean something, and even taking back your partner after breaking up—can all serve as an attempt to end or at least slow down an escalation. But in the end, it's your partner who's in control and determines how far the escalation will go.

Physical violence toward you by an intimate partner is clearly dangerous. It's also illegal, and such behaviors are criminal acts. At the same time, women don't always take seriously the physical violence they experience. Here are some of the ways you might minimize or deny it:

- You think it's an isolated incident and it won't happen again

- If it does happen again, you feel—or are made to feel— responsible

- You start paying more attention to trying to prevent your partner from escalating to physical violence

Foremost, feeling depleted by psychological abuse makes it harder for you to take steps to protect yourself at times of physical violence. You are scared, confused, and now further traumatized by the physical attack. Keep in the forefront of your mind that you're not the cause, but the recipient of his abuse. He's solely responsible for his violent behavior, and it's unacceptable and wrong, in every way.

# Impact of Physical Violence

Clearly, physical violence can cause physical injuries of all sorts—like stab wounds, broken bones, and traumatic brain injuries—and ultimately even cause death. Injuries are serious, can be life-threatening, and need attention. Some controlling partners refuse to allow their partners to seek medical help, putting them at even greater risk of an even more serious nature. In addition, many adverse physical health conditions are recognized as resulting from the impact of intimate partner violence that profoundly affects your life. Centers for Disease Control and Prevention reports (CDC 2008) that women who have experienced domestic violence are:

- 80 percent more likely to have a stroke

- 70 percent more likely to have heart disease

- 60 percent more likely to have asthma

- 70 percent more likely to drink heavily.

While these statistics show that your physical health can suffer, it is just one of the many ways you experience loss with a controlling partner. Violence not only impacts your physical health, but also your emotional and psychological well-being. In addition, when you're already experiencing psychological abuse and then encounter physical violence, the traumatic impact is exacerbated and made worse. In the person being targeted, physical violence creates confusion, fear, anxiety, depression, suicidal ideation and behavior, low self-esteem, sleep disturbances, and post-traumatic stress disorder.

Those who witness the violence and threats of violence, such as friends, family members, and children, are also psychologically impacted. One in fifteen children annually are exposed to intimate partner violence, with 90 percent of these children being eyewitnesses to the violence (Hamby et al. 2011). Living with threats and acts of physical violence leaves you (and your children) feeling unsafe because you're not safe. Getting safe has to be a priority to work toward in your recovery.

## Looking at Your Own Relationship

Right now, if any situation described in this chapter relates to your experience, you might be struggling with letting yourself fully see it and embrace it for what it is. While you're likely to have more aware-ness of the physical abuse your partner uses against you, like psycho-logical abuse, physical violence also gets minimized and denied. Psychologically abused women say, "If he'd hit me, then I'd know it's wrong and I could leave." But it's not that clear when you're in the throes of an intimate relationship with physical violence. It's never okay for someone to physically hurt you or threaten to hurt you. You don't deserve this, no matter what has occurred beforehand. Your behavior does not give him license to be physically violent. Controlling partners are known to accuse their partners of attacking first when, in reality, women are defending themselves. (Remember that defending yourself doesn't stop the abuse and only places you at greater risk for injury.) Don't be persuaded to believe in any way that you're responsi-ble, as you now turn to your own experience and record what happened.

### EXERCISE: Is Your Partner Physically Violent?

If you experience physical violence, you need to start taking it seriously, if you have not already. It's important to prioritize your safety, so start by taking to heart how he harms you. Answer the following questions: Is your partner physically abusive or violent? If so, what does he do?

In your journal, write down specifically what your partner does in a physical way that hurts you. Make a list of each incident with a description of what occurred and a date, or approximate date, of when it happened. You can revisit the "Controlling Behavior Checklist" you completed in chapter 3 to see what you identified as physical violence. The information and lists offered earlier in this chapter can also help you along.

Write about what your partner does that scares, hurts, or injures you. Recognize how you feel and, most importantly, to what degree you feel you're in danger of physical violence going forward. Creating a safety plan, so you have helpful options at these moments, is definitely in your best interest. It's almost impossible to fully recover and be at your strongest without feeling safe. I'll say more about safety plans after we address sexual violence.

## Sexual Violence

Sexual violence or abuse in an intimate relationship is an act of violence—not sex—that's used by a controlling partner to achieve dominance and power over you. Sexual violence is an area of serious abuse that gets far too little attention and recognition. I'll begin with an explanation of what is meant by sexual violence, as it is defined by the National Center for Injury Prevention and Control (a division of CDC). Sexual violence has three different types that include:

- Any use of physical force to make another person "engage in a sexual act unwillingly," irrespective of whether that sexual act is completed.

- A sexual act, either attempted or completed, that involves a person who—due to a disability, an illness, or under the influence of alcohol or other drugs, or because of pressure or intimidation—is unable to realize the nature of the sexual act, or refuse participation, or is unable to communicate an unwillingness to participate in the sexual act.

- Abusive sexual contact that includes unwanted sexual contact. (CDC 2016)

Statistics are revealing and help us recognize the serious occurrence of sexual violence in intimate relationships in the United States. For example, between 40 and 45 percent of women in abusive relationships will also be sexually assaulted; sexual coercion, which is unwanted intercourse after being pressured nonphysically, is experienced by 13 percent of women during their lives. At the same time, marital rape, when compared to all sexual assaults, is the most underreported. Six times as many women victimized by an intimate partner (18 percent) compared to those victimized by a stranger (3 percent) claimed their fear of retaliation by their partner kept them from reporting to the police (CDC 2010).

Women in recovery often report feeling so intimidated by their partner's anger, putdowns, threats, or unrelenting pressure to have sex that they finally give in to make him stop—only to be left feeling horrible about what they went through. Sexual abuse and violence within an intimate relationship, which is often a marriage, creates enormous shame that makes it extremely difficult to discuss openly, whether in a recovery group or not, and to report it to authorities may feel impossible. I hope to help you recognize sexual abuse if you experience it; move out of minimizing it, whether you do so because of your shame or society's expectations; and ultimately learn ways to protect yourself.

It's important for you to know that research shows sexual assault by an intimate partner is found to be just as physically brutal, if not more, and psychologically as damaging as sexual assault by a stranger (Logan, Cole, and Capillo 2007; Basile et al. 2004). Yet, the general public views sexual assault by an intimate partner as a lesser crime than assault by a stranger. And the general public tends to see the victim responsible, which clearly adds to the denial of sexual abuse by an intimate partner. This makes it difficult for women, perhaps like yourself, to believe they can take their sexual abuse seriously, step forward to seek help, and receive protection. Don't let society's distorted perspective contribute to your view and *do* take seriously your sexual abuse. You are not responsible and it's horrific for anyone to believe otherwise.

## Acts That Constitute Sexual Abuse

From the women in recovery groups, it's clear that it's hard to share experiences of sexual violence. The deep shame and humiliation that results causes many women not to speak to anyone about it or seek help. When it can be talked about, a somber atmosphere emerges. It's scary and sad to hear and realize the horrific abuse that some women endure.

One woman endured sexual assault and threats that led her to participate in sexual acts that left her feeling deeply embarrassed and ashamed. When she came to the group, she cried the whole time she told her story. Another woman who faced similar abuse never showed up for the group. If she had, she would have seen that she is not alone and that the sexual violence is not her fault. She would have felt understood—an important step toward reducing the painful shame that keeps women like her isolated. To help you begin to open up about your experience and know you're not alone, here is a list of acts that constitute sexual abuse that women in recovery have reported. For now, recognize those experiences that resonate with your own.

- Threatening and coercing you to have sex with him, to have sex when he wants it, or to have sex you don't like. You acquiesce under the intimidation and pressure.

- Coercing or threatening you to have sex involving others.

- Demanding sex because he believes it's his right.

- Making you perform sex acts to get things you or your children may need or want.

- Touching or attacking sexual parts of your body when you don't want him to.

- Making degrading sexual comments or treating you in a sexually demeaning way.

- Waking up to find your partner attempting to have sex with you.

- Using physical force to make you engage a sexual act against your will—which is rape, according to the law.

## Impact of Sexual Violence

Women who are sexually abused by an intimate partner have long-lasting mental and physical health issues, not unlike victims of rape by a stranger. We also know from research that these women experience a higher rate of depression and anxiety than women who are physically abused, but not sexually abused, by their intimate partner (Bergen and Barnhill 2006). In addition, there are more risk factors identified for homicide for sexually abused women (McFarlane and Malecha 2005).

## Looking at Your Own Relationship

When it comes to sexual violence by an intimate partner, although difficult to talk about and easily minimized or denied by our culture and individuals, it's critical for you to take it seriously. Sexual violence tells you that your intimate partner has the potential to possibly ratchet up his abuse and increase your injuries even to a lethal level.

I imagine this is frightening, but it's the reality of what we know, so be sure to look at your experience head-on because honesty will help you the most going forward. You don't deserve sexual abuse or coercion and, whether you're married or not, you have the right to make your own sexual choices. Keep this in mind as you turn to look at your own experience.

### EXERCISE: Is Your Partner Sexually Abusive?

This is a journaling exercise during which you might find it difficult to sit with the feelings that arise. Feel free to stop if you need to, or to work on it for only short periods of time.

In a quiet place with your journal handy, settle into yourself. Take a few deep breaths. When you're ready, focus on your sexual experience with your partner. As best as you can, list the times when you have been: coerced to have sex to get things you may need or want, for yourself or your children; pressured, intimidated, or threatened to have sex or sex you don't like; physically forced to have sex. Describe what happened in each scenario and identify if rape occurred. Yes, being physically forced to have sex is rape. Keep this important record in a safe place. If you choose at some future time to seek legal help and protection, this information can be useful.

## Building Internal Resistance: Planning for Safety

Just to reiterate: you are not responsible in any way for your partner's threats or physical or sexual violence. You cannot make him say hurtful threats or do harm to you. These are his choices and only his to own. You deserve to be treated respectfully and to expect that for yourself. At a time of urgency when you feel terrified, and unsafe, you can call 911 and let the dispatcher know that you're scared and in danger. If you're unable to get to a phone, leave and go to a public place to seek help. Planning for your safety ahead of time—as much as you can—is always in your best interest.

Safety planning, a critical part of your recovery, is a process that helps you determine how to keep yourself safer at times you're in danger of physical or sexual violence from your controlling partner. You determine ahead of time the steps that you can take to help you minimize or avoid his harm to you.

The best way to obtain help with safety planning is to contact one of the many domestic violence hotlines to address your specific situation. The domestic violence advocate can provide information, support services, legal advocacy, and another perspective to think through your situation with you. You don't have to do this alone. Reaching out to an advocate in a domestic violence program helps you reduce the isolation you might be experiencing while getting help and support—as many times as you might need it. They are not there to tell you what to do, as they recognize that you're the expert of your situation. In a blog post titled "Safety Planning: An Advocate's Perspective," one advocate wrote:

> When I'm talking with survivors, it often becomes clear that it's not always possible to create a "safe" situation. Our focus has to be on making it safer. I ask questions, help them think through the situation, think of alternatives just in case, and we try to create a plan to reduce the potential harm and keep them as safe as possible. We know that we can't control an abuser's behavior, and the safety plan isn't intended to place responsibility on the survivor, but to give that person as much agency as possible over the things they can control. (REACH 2014)

For guidance with safety planning, visit The National Domestic Violence Hotline website (www.thehotline.org) and search specifically for "safety planning." If you're visiting websites and your partner is around, there's an "escape" button on the top of the screen for a quick exit. As I mentioned before, if you suspect your partner looks at your browsing history and other information on your computer, you might go to your local library to use a computer. Or, even better if you can, make a call to The National Domestic Violence Hotline at 800-799-7233. All calls are confidential and anonymous. You'll reach a person who is trained and skilled with safety planning and can help you put together a workable safety plan for yourself and your children. They can also tell you about "emergency escape plans" for you to have if necessary. In addition, they provide safety planning for family members, friends, and for children—with helpful guidance on how to talk to children.

## Check-In

Threats and physical and sexual violence are extremely traumatizing to the targeted person. As I mentioned earlier, the intensity of acute abuse occurs in Phase 2 of the cycle of abuse, leaving you feeling trapped and terrified. I encourage you to use the exercises and grounding techniques outlined in chapter 7 to address the different trauma reactions that you might find yourself experiencing. These strategies can help you move through your reactions.

## You've Got This!

When your partner becomes physically or sexually violent or makes threats of physical harm, you are in danger. His behavior, at these times, is recognized as criminal and you have options for legal protection. You may or may not want to call the police, but it's important for you to know that you can. Having a safety plan and an emergency escape plan in place helps you to be ready to take steps to protect yourself (and your children) at these dangerous times. In the meantime, having these plans developed and in hand can help you feel more in control of your life.

# CHAPTER 11

# Recognize Your Injuries
# from Abuse

You have continued your recovery and, as a result, you are far more aware and knowledgeable about the abusive experience with your controlling partner. You deserve to be treated so much better than what you are getting. And I imagine your recovery is helping you recognize that. Right now, your recovery is great self-care. Good for you!

We finish Stage Two by addressing the last two coercive tactics. At first, you might be surprised to see that these are coercive tactics. The first does not seem to be negative because it has to do with the good times you share with your partner. The second appears to be more of an effect of traumatic abuse than a tactic. Yet they are both powerful coercive influences that contribute significantly to your partner having control over your life. The two coercive tactics discussed here are:

- Occasional indulgences
- Induced debility and trauma

## Controlling Tactic: Occasional Indulgences

Occasional indulgences happen when your partner turns nice after being abusive. At these times, he can be attentive and caring, and make promises for a better future. You're likely to hope that the two of you can have a better relationship. His caring interaction becomes proof that he can behave in a better way—the way you had hoped he would be with you. Although all of this may feel wonderful in the moment, it's not the truth. He's not being genuine, instead he's manipulating and seducing you back into the relationship. The favorable behavior that shows up after an abusive episode is the powerful coercive tactic of occasional indulgences. Recognizing and accepting the truth behind what he falsely presents as good intentions might be the biggest challenge for you in your recovery.

To understand the manipulative quality of his good behavior in the context of controlling relationships, we need to circle back to the cycle of abuse in chapter 7, specifically to Phase 3—the reconciliation and honeymoon phase. During Phase 3 of the abuse cycle, your partner's behavior can become kind and even loving. This positive behavior follows Phase 2, the acute abuse phase, in which intense psychological or physical violence takes place. While you are experiencing severe abusive attacks, you're not in denial—rather you are completely aware of his mistreatment. You feel upset, hurt, and might even see him as a monster. A controlling partner must then consciously draw you back into his fold with the use of positive behaviors—the behaviors he believes will successfully convince you.

When your partner changes to "nice," it's because he senses you have pulled away following the horrific abuse. This threatens him, so in order to address what happened, he may apologize and profess it won't happen again with such loving conviction that it feels believable—so you find yourself capitulating. You might even feel better about yourself during this phase, since these moments of care can offer boosts of good feelings and self-esteem that counter the emotional pain of feeling so devalued and hurt.

Revisiting Jen's story in chapter 7 will remind you how this plays out. Her husband was upset because when he got home from work she and the kids were not there. Jen had gone to the park with her children but returned alone to the house while her children stayed with a friend. Upon hearing her, her husband rushed into the kitchen, cornered her, and raged on and on about what a terrible mother she was. This occurred during Phase 2 of the cycle of abuse where, in this case,

Jen felt trapped and terrified by her husband's intensely abusive attacks. The next morning, Jen's husband had shifted to the coercive tactic known as occasional indulgences—Phase 3 of the cycle. She found him in the kitchen making funny-face pancakes with the kids, preparing to bring her breakfast in bed. Later he apologized, telling her it wouldn't happen again. Her husband's behavior became more attentive and apologetic, weakening Jen's resolve.

These occasional indulgences of positive attention, caring behaviors, gifts, or apologies provide positive reasons for the person targeted to go along and be persuaded by the controlling partner—especially after a serious abusive episode. Clearly, it feels so much better to feel cared for. And in a relationship that diminishes self-esteem, this caring behavior leads you to feel good about yourself, making this manipulation all the more powerful. When this occurs over and over, it can instill in you the practice of compliance on a deeper level. Ultimately, your partner keeps you entrapped in the relationship.

## Looking at Your Own Relationship

When your partner's behavior turns nice following an abusive episode, it is a tactic to lower your resistance to him—I can't stress this enough. It may seem like a powerful time of caring, and your heart wants to believe all will be well. However, it never stays that way because he will revert back to his explicitly controlling ways.

You need to separate what's real from what's a maneuver to win you over. For his behavior to truly be a lasting and positive change, your partner would need to take full responsibility for his abuse and believe you are not at fault in any way for his use of abuse. He would need to fully own his hurtful behavior over time and have deep feelings of remorse and care about the painful effects his abuse has had on you and the children. In most cases, this would require him to want to change and no longer be controlling and abusive. To accomplish this, he would need to be willing to seek help and follow through. Without this sincere stance, his favorable behavior following abuse is a manipulation that will recur again and again.

## EXERCISE: "Nice" Behavior Is Meant to Seduce You

This exercise is designed to help you examine times of occasional indulgences and determine if your partner is manipulating you. Following are four questions. Use the scale that follows to indicate your response to each statement.

1—Strongly disagree

2—Somewhat disagree

3—Feel neutral

4—Somewhat agree

5—Strongly agree

Record your responses to these statements:

- After my partner abuses me, he gives me positive attention.

- My partner tries to convince me that he didn't really mean the hurtful things he said or did.

- I believe or want to believe my partner when he apologizes for his abusive reactions—he appears so sincere.

- My partner has made promises to change many times, but he never does.

Take a look at your responses.

If you scored between 13 and 16, you need to pay attention to the possibility of being manipulated.

If you scored between 16 and 20, you have a clear indication that your partner manipulates you with the use of occasional indulgences.

# Building Resistance to Occasional Indulgences

If you're persuaded by his nice behavior and the occasional indulgences, you then have no choice but to deny the abuse that came before and is likely to come after. In order to protect yourself from falling for this coercive tactic, and see "nice" for the manipulation it is, you need to keep his abuse in your consciousness at all times. Here are some ways to help yourself stay grounded in a realistic perception of your partner.

Make a point to journal about these specific transitions from Phase 2 to Phase 3—from acute abuse to occasional indulgences. First, describe the abusive episode that came before your partner turned nice. Then, identify the occasional indulgences—his positive behaviors—and how they make you feel. See how they invite you to feel hopeful, which requires you to overlook the abuse. That's when you're misled. Documenting this transition when it happens, in real time, will help you recognize this coercive tactic in action for the manipulation it is.

In your journal, make note of how long his nice behavior, including the calm period, lasts. Then become aware of what follows in the cycle of abuse: when you're back walking in a minefield as he shows tension-building behavior. Phase 3 never lasts, and all too soon you will be back in Phase 1 of the cycle of abuse.

Revisit your responses to the exercises in chapter 7 when you looked at your experience during the phases. In particular, review how in Phase 2 you are fully aware and impacted by his severe abuse and then, when his nice behavior follows in Phase 3, you're drawn back into denying or minimizing the abuse that occurred.

To stay aware of his abuse, particularly when he turns nice, you can always remind yourself by revisiting your "Controlling Behavior Checklist" from chapter 3 where you checked off your partner's abusive behaviors.

As you work to develop a realistic perception of your partner—including his seemingly nice behavior that's not so nice anymore—you may feel sadness and grief as you experience a loss of hope for your relationship. This awareness can instigate mourning for the relationship you imagined you could eventually have. What you gain, however, is trust in what's realistic, which works in your favor as you boost confidence to act in your own best interest.

EXERCISE: Your Courtship Revisited

When women experience favorable behavior and occasional indulgences, they often feel they are back with the man they fell in love with. This takes them back to how their partner behaved during their courtship. In chapter 5, you had an opportunity to think about the dating experience with your partner and record a list of behaviors that showed what he was like during that time.

Because you are now armed with knowledge of what makes up the coercive tactics, you can recognize early signs of control that you most likely were previously unaware of. I'd like you to revisit the information you wrote in your journal about your dating experience and indicate which behaviors would meet the definition of a coercive tactic, if any. When you identify one, circle it or flag it with a red mark. I like to think of this as a final exam of sorts, and you can do this now.

Feel free to review the coercive tactics to feel more confident while making these assessments. What's most important is identifying the coercive tactics as they first appeared while dating. If you come up with none, then you know that your partner made sure not to reveal any of his controlling tendencies. If you find some, this exercise will help you see that you can now recognize controlling behavior.

## Controlling Tactic: Induced Debility and Trauma

Occasional indulgences as well as isolation, monopolization of perception, devaluation and humiliation, claiming superiority, enforcing trivial demands, and threats cause a decline in your mental and physical health. These tactics diminish who you are: your sense of competence, your drive and ambition, and your mastery and control over your life. Stress-related symptoms such as headaches, numbness, exhaustion, and loss of memory begin to show up. Ultimately, your partner's abuse weakens you, making it *harder to resist him*. You end up being more dependent on the very person who does not look out for your best interest. Induced debility or trauma is the eighth and final coercive tactic—and it is powerful. For you to know the ways that debilitation or trauma manifests in you not only gives you clear conviction of the depth of his harmful control, it also provides insight into how you can restore your health.

It is time to confront the serious ramifications of your partner's abuse on both your physical and mental health. In chapter 1, research showed us the serious impact of psychological abuse. In chapter 10, we looked at the negative effects of physical and sexual violence, and threats of it. In all my years of working with women in my groups, I have never seen anyone escape injury. It is simply not possible to be mistreated by an intimate partner and not experience some wounds. Whatever abuse you've endured, your thoughts, feelings, and body are affected and that impinges on your overall functioning. Over time, with a controlling partner you are no longer as strong, as confident, nor as content as you once were. It's the decline—your worn-down state or debilitation—that adds to feeling vulnerable and can cause you to feel incapable of protecting yourself.

Annabelle, a forty-five-year-old mother of two children in middle school, shared that she noticed she was drinking more wine than usual, and that it seemed to start around dinner time when her husband was expected to come home. She knew this was not good for her, yet she felt she didn't know what else to do. Annabelle added, "I can't settle down my body—I'm so anxious and stressed all the time. Drinking wine is the only thing that seems to help."

At this point in your recovery, we move from looking at controlling behavior and hidden injuries to looking at the resulting traumatic impact. It's time to pay particularly close attention to how you feel, to your beliefs about yourself, and to what you physically experience in your body. From there, you can generate a list of the hidden injuries and traumatic effects that you experience. Here is a list of symptoms from one group of women in recovery. You might find yourself experiencing some of the same symptoms.

- Anxiety and panic
- Confusion
- Decline in the care of your home
- Decline in work performance
- Depression
- Exhaustion
- Fear
- Financial worries
- Headaches
- Helplessness
- High blood pressure
- Hurting yourself
- Insomnia
- Lack of control
- Less social contact
- Loss of confidence
- Low self-esteem
- Nightmares
- Overeating
- Post-traumatic stress
- Sadness
- Suicidal thoughts
- Under eating
- Worries about the children

This list shows the severe impact of psychological abuse, clearly and profoundly. None of these women experienced physical violence. Like these women, you need to take seriously any injuries caused by your partner's controlling tactics that, before your recovery, were unseen and unknown to you.

You've carried the burden of these wounds. In the fog and confusion, you could not make out why your lives were not right and why you didn't feel okay. Now, by identifying the traumatic impact of your partner's abuse, you can see how you've been hurt on many levels and know what needs to heal.

## Looking at Your Own Relationship

You now have the opportunity to look at yourself to see what you have been living with as the result of your partner's controlling tactics. You will benefit by recognizing how you've been affected, as it provides a window into how to get stronger.

### EXERCISE: Identify Your Wounds from Abuse

With your journal, find a quiet place. Once you're settled, start with what you're aware of within yourself. Generate your own list of symptoms and conditions. Identify any injuries, either psychological or physical. While you do this exercise, you may become aware of increasingly more disturbing symptoms—but this does not mean that you're crazy. On the contrary, you are on your way to becoming clearheaded.

Your list is a good start to paying attention to the impact of your partner's control on your emotional and physical health. To assist you further, I will next provide a checklist that includes symptoms that have been identified in the field of domestic violence as a result of the various types of abuse we've reviewed.

## EXERCISE: Traumatic Effects of Abuse Checklist

The traumatic effects experienced by women who are, or have been, in a relationship with a controlling partner can include any or all of the following psychological responses or adaptations to traumatic occurrences (Coker et al. 2000; Dutton 1992; APA 2013). Put an "X" beside the symptoms you are currently experiencing. Put a "P" beside the symptoms you have experienced in the past, but no longer experience. If you have never experienced the symptom, leave the space blank.

### Mental Health Conditions

☐ Fear or terror

### Intrusive Symptoms

☐ Body sensations (having a physical sense that may not have a clear cause in the moment)

☐ Dissociative reactions such as flashbacks (when you feel or act as if the abusive episode is recurring)

☐ Distressing affective responses (emotionally overreacting to something that doesn't warrant the reaction but triggers the abuse trauma)

☐ Intense and prolonged psychological distress, either within you or externally, that's associated with some aspect of the abuse

☐ Recurring, distressful dreams that hold themes or emotions related to the abuse

☐ Recurring, distressful memories of the abuse

### Avoidance Responses

☐ Avoiding, or striving to avoid, external reminders that bring up distressing memories, thoughts, or feelings that you associate with the abuse

☐ Constriction of affect (not feeling your full range of feelings)

☐ Persistent avoidance of memories, thoughts, or feelings associated with the abuse

## Changes in Mood and Cognition

☐ Loss of interest and involvement in important activities

☐ Loss of memory for important aspects of the abuse

☐ Ongoing negative emotions like fear, terror, shame, or guilt

☐ Persistent and intense negative beliefs or expectations about yourself or others

☐ Persistent feelings of being detached from others; experiencing dissociation (you perceive yourself as an outside observer of yourself)

☐ Persistent inability to experience positive feelings such as joy or satisfaction

☐ Persistent, distorted beliefs about the cause or result of the abuse that lead to blaming yourself

## Arousal Reactions

☐ Difficulty concentrating

☐ Hypervigilance

☐ Outbursts of anger, rage, or hostility for little or no reason

☐ Problems falling asleep or staying asleep

☐ Self-destructive behavior

☐ Severe startle responses

## Other Psychological Responses

☐ Anorexia

☐ Anxiety

☐ Compulsive busyness such as housecleaning

☐ Compulsive gambling

☐ Compulsive or binge eating, including bulimia

☐ Compulsive spending and shopping

☐ Confusion, feeling like you are in a fog

☐ Depression

☐ Fear of going crazy

☐ Grief and sadness

☐ Homicidal intent

☐ Impaired ability to socialize

☐ Impaired functioning as a parent

☐ Impaired work performance

☐ Inability to trust you will not be physically or emotionally hurt in other relationships

☐ Loss of interest in or desire for previously enjoyed activities such as sex

☐ Low self-esteem or feeling unworthy

☐ Morbid hatred or homicidal thoughts

☐ Panic

☐ Self-mutilation, including cutting

☐ Severe depression with feelings of hopelessness

☐ Shame or feeling inferior

☐ Substance abuse (alcohol or drugs that include prescription medications)

☐ Suicidal thoughts

☐ Suicide attempts

## Physical Health Conditions

- ☐ Chronic fatigue
- ☐ Headaches
- ☐ Issues with menstrual cycle or fertility
- ☐ Lower-back pain
- ☐ Nausea
- ☐ Sexual dysfunction
- ☐ Shaking, trembling
- ☐ Shortness of breath
- ☐ Stomachaches

## Adverse Health Problems (Coker et al. 2000)

- ☐ Arthritis
- ☐ Chronic pain
- ☐ Chronic pelvic pain
- ☐ Migraines or frequent headaches
- ☐ Sexually transmitted infections
- ☐ Spastic colon
- ☐ Stammering
- ☐ Stomach ulcers

It's important to keep in mind that these responses are the traumatic effects of being in an abusive relationship. Anyone with an abusive partner can be at risk for developing these physical and mental health conditions.

Now that you've completed the checklist, you can see the multiple ways that you have been affected by your partner's controlling behavior. If it's been hard to take 100 percent of his abuse seriously, I hope

your symptoms will give you the final push to move out of any minimizing or denying to fully embrace the very serious nature of all your
partner's abusive behavior.

## Understand Your Symptoms

Let's turn to your responses in the checklist that you completed. As I
mentioned in chapter 1, depression, anxiety, low self-esteem, and post-
traumatic stress disorder are conditions you're at risk of having if you
are with a partner who uses psychological abuse. These conditions are
intensified if you also endure threats of harm or physical and sexual
violence. Obviously, if you checked "Fear or terror," you are not feeling
safe. Chronic fear and terror propel trauma and symptoms of trauma.
Eventually, finding ways to feel safe, or safer, will be important and
necessary for a full recovery.

It's important to know that women who experience, or have a
history of experiencing, domestic violence or intimate partner violence are more likely to show behaviors that put them at increased
health risks. These include more substance abuse, alcoholism, and
suicide attempts than women who have no experience with abuse by
an intimate partner. In fact, of the women who experience domestic
violence, one out of four attempt suicide (Caruso 2016). Research also
shows us that, as the severity of violence increases, there is a greater
possibility that the targeted person will participate in negative health-
risk behaviors (Plichta 2004).

EXERCISE: See Your Traumatic Effects

Here is a brief journaling exercise. With your journal available, focus
on your reaction to what you just learned, especially your feelings. The
following questions may guide you.

- How does learning about your symptoms make you feel
  about your partner and relationship?

- Are you feeling any anger or sadness for the hurt and pain
  he has caused you?

- Do your feelings motivate you to tackle what you need to do in order to help yourself feel better?

- If not, what gets in the way of feeling motivated to help yourself?

You cannot live normally or ever be at your best when your partner's abuse negatively alters your feelings, thoughts, and behavior. The good news is that your recovery is helping you change that. Knowing your symptoms gives you a wealth of information about what you need to attend to so you can keep moving forward.

## Understand Your Trauma Response

First of all, it can feel daunting to recognize the depth of hurt your partner's behavior has caused you. At the same time, knowing how badly you feel, a part of you may find this new information validating and encouraging, since it gives you a direction for how to feel better. Even by accomplishing what you have in your recovery so far, your symptoms could be fewer, or less intense, than when you started this process. Although women with controlling partners all have a similar experience, how you respond to the trauma from the abuse you endured is unique.

Looking at your own experience of abuse, many factors can influence the degree of traumatic impact you experience. How we handle stress in our lives varies; some of us have learned better coping strategies than others. The severity, intensity, frequency, and length of time the abusive episodes have lasted all strongly impact your response as well. Other powerful influences include the length of time your personal traumatic reaction lasts after your partner's abuse stops and your history, before you ever met your partner.

Some women are more vulnerable to getting involved with a controlling partner because of past traumatic experiences. However, remember that not all women who are "susceptible" end up with a controlling partner. Likewise, women without trauma or abuse in their past and with healthy self-esteem can find themselves with a partner who controls and abuses them as well. It's in your best interest to get clear about the ways you might be vulnerable.

We have learned from domestic violence and trauma experts (Dutton 1992; van der Kolk 2014) that certain past traumatic experiences and physical and mental conditions can make you more susceptible to a partner's coercive tactics. Past traumatic events that can make you more susceptible include:

- Physical or sexual abuse during your childhood

- Witnessing violence, such as your mother being abused

- Physical or sexual abuse and violence by a stranger, a date, or a person in authority such as a teacher, boss, or coach

- A chaotic childhood home life caused by the early loss of a parent or growing up with an alcoholic parent

- Having a mental or physical disability

No one deserves to be abused, so don't confuse vulnerability with cause for being abused. The factors that make you susceptible can, but do not always, make it harder to protect yourself. If you are susceptible and never had a prior trauma treated, you could find your partner's mistreatment harder to recognize. In chapter 14, "Moving Forward—What Do You Want?" we'll address what to do about the unfinished hurt from the past.

It's important for those of you who live with children to know the harmful impact of psychological abuse, physical violence, and threats on young witnesses between the ages of three and seventeen. They can see, hear, notice aftermaths, and experience ongoing tension in their home. They can sense their mother's stress and the negative changes in her demeanor that can happen with specific events, like their father arriving home.

In this environment, children are anxious, afraid, and can stay vigilant about what might happen next. Not having the luxury of a safe home, they are left to worry about their mother, themselves, and siblings. In the end, they can feel what you feel—profound powerlessness. And we know children in a home with abuse are much more likely to be abused themselves. Your children will greatly benefit from your recovery because it puts you in a stronger position to help them—an important incentive for you to keep moving forward. In the Resources section, you will find helpful places to turn for support for your children.

## Check-In

Recognizing your injuries from your partner's mistreatment may feel daunting. At the same time, find comfort in knowing that what you do know now and have accomplished so far is all in the service of your healing and strengthening. Keep up with coping the best you can; remind yourself to engage in self-care and use the techniques from chapter 7 to manage your painful emotions as you need to.

## You've Got This!

A controlling partner uses occasional indulgences, in the form of positive behavior following abuse, to manipulate you into believing in his good intentions and to persuade you to overlook the abuse. When you stay grounded in the reality of your partner's abusiveness, you can negate the hope and boost of self-esteem that his caring behavior can temporarily generate in you. By doing so, you take a step toward your best interest—which is healthy self-esteem—and away from his powerful manipulation and control.

We have completed the last coercive tactic of induced debility or trauma. The "Traumatic Effects of Abuse Checklist" gave you a clear picture of how you are impacted by your partner's abuse. By now, you must be fairly certain that you cannot feel good or be at your best when exposed to ongoing psychological abuse and possibly physical or sexual violence. However, it is possible for you to recover from the symptoms you identified, including post-traumatic stress disorder. Continuing your recovery work in the next chapter marks the beginning of Stage Three.

STAGE THREE

# Reclaim Yourself—
# Only You Know
# What's Best for You

# CHAPTER 12

# Change Beliefs to Feel Stronger

Congratulations! You have completed Stage Two of your recovery. We covered a lot of ground in that stage, beginning with dating a controlling partner and his tendency to conceal abusive control. Then we saw the commitment stage, when he took control in little and big ways—trapping you in the relationship. Next we looked at the cycle of abuse and how the changes in your partner's behavior create a distinct pattern that perpetuates the abusive relationship. Then we identified six coercive tactics embedded in your partner's behavior that have serious hidden injuries, before moving on to how to recognize threats and physical and sexual violence. Finally, we identified the coercive tactic of debilitation—the traumatic impact of all of this on your mental and physical health. From the start of your recovery, you have been learning ways to deconstruct the psychological entrapment created by your partner's control so you can take back yourself.

Laura, a domestic violence survivor, wrote a meaningful and moving story about her recovery titled, "The Monster Story." To begin our work together in Stage Three, I'm providing part of the third segment. The story, in its entirety, is available online at the following link: http://www.newharbinger.com/34718.

> As she watched the monster sleep, something inside of her started to change. Her pity, helplessness, and fear began to fade. And her courage, self-preservation, and anger began to grow. She finally saw him as he was—a monster. He was not the loving man he pretended to be at first. Although she felt stronger, she was still afraid...so, very quietly, she began to peel away at the inside of the box...

Suddenly, it came to her. She was not really trapped at all. This was an illusion the monster had created to keep her near him. She smiled out of relief as she realized that the box she was in could not hold the strong woman she had uncovered.

Let's recognize that you, too, have been peeling away at the inside of a box. You've worked hard *and* stuck with it. You tackled an enormous problem you have with your partner that you might have sensed but did not clearly see until now. You know so much more about this stressful experience, the complicated feelings you have, and the repetitive difficulties you encounter with him. Throughout your recovery, it has taken effort and courage to persevere to this point. Be proud of that! I'm excited for you—even though I don't know you by name, I do know you by your experience. This is not who you are so much as what you're going through or went through in your past. What you've accomplished so far has given you a life-changing foundation with new direction to build on for yourself, and possibly for your relationship.

This chapter marks the beginning of Stage Three. To continue building on your newfound knowledge and strength, we'll work to recommit to positive beliefs and address the negative beliefs that have resulted from your partner's coercion. These negative beliefs, if left unattended, will continue to reinforce his control over you. To defend against your partner's control, you need to believe and trust in yourself. After this, in chapter 13, you'll recognize what makes a successful relationship, revisit your goals to identify what you want, and understand your options with a controlling partner going forward.

## Take Stock of Your Present Self

Psychological abuse by a controlling partner has targeted your thoughts, feelings, and perceptions. As a result of your partner's psychological abuse and brainwashing, you developed negative beliefs and feelings about yourself that have suppressed the good things you feel about yourself, or at least did feel in the past. One particular area called *Changes in Mood and Cognition,* from the "Traumatic Effects of Abuse Checklist" offered in chapter 11, revealed negative conditions that can result from your partner's abuse. These include: hurtful beliefs about yourself; distorted beliefs about what causes the abuse which leads to blaming yourself; and harmful feelings such as fear, shame, or guilt. This is what we're now working on to begin undoing.

Brainwashing results in changed beliefs and it occurs in a situation with close and ongoing influence (Taylor 2004). We know from our work so far that "close and ongoing influence" is central to what controlling partners create in their intimate relationships. Taylor addresses ways to bolster resistance to brainwashing and offers the following useful approaches to defusing it.

- Make a commitment to center yourself in beliefs that are incompatible with the messages you receive from your partner's abusive accusations, and increase this commitment over time.

- Reduce any beliefs you have that support your partner's accusations and reduce the negative feelings you have that make his accusations and beliefs powerful.

- Change your current beliefs or create new beliefs to reflect your own thoughts and feelings.

The more you commit to strong beliefs about yourself, the more you defend yourself against brainwashing. Ultimately, with an abusive partner, once his coercion declines or is gone, your previous thoughts and feelings can emerge (Taylor 2004).

# Turning the Corner: Hold Your Partner Responsible for His Coercion

Controlling partners are experts at blaming their partners. When your partner blames you over and over again, with strong conviction and convincing arguments, you can end up assuming that blame. This results in cognitive and emotional changes. You internalize his false accusations and develop negative beliefs about yourself—we've reviewed the ways he accomplishes this, both explicitly and implicitly.

This comes at a big cost to you and now we need to make sure that you can rid yourself of any lingering self-blame for his abuse.

Blaming yourself causes you to feel painful shame, guilt, and even self-hatred in the extreme. These negative feelings contribute to anxiety, depression, suicidal thoughts, and low self-worth. Remember, your self-blame is developed from your partner's verbal attacks and distortions of the truth. You cannot make him abuse you and you cannot make him not abuse you. He's in control of his own actions and words. When you fully see that his coercion is a choice he makes, you'll turn the corner and stop assuming blame. This is what Lucy experienced during her recovery.

Lucy was a fifty-three-year-old woman who was married for twenty-eight years. While in recovery, she learned about the coercive tactics used by her partner and the serious impact on her own health. At one point, she became angry and even furious, but unfortunately it was all toward herself. She was upset that she didn't see what was taking place, didn't stop it, didn't prevent it—and that she hadn't left. Initially, Lucy could not see how her self-blame was a result of her husband's blame, but now she was criticizing herself.

When Lucy fully recognized what she was doing, it helped her turn the corner and hold her husband solely responsible for all his abuse. Then, a remarkable thing happened. She felt much lighter, got her glow back, and her great sense of humor returned. Lucy discovered that feeling angry about the abuse was actually energizing and gave her fuel to assert what she wanted for herself. She took steps to divorce her husband.

Sometimes we can come to *believe* something to be true before we can also *feel* that it's true. For change to happen, both need to take place. To this point, after all you learned, you may truly believe that your partner's abuse is terribly wrong and deeply unfair. To hold him responsible for his abuse, let yourself be aware of how you *feel* about what he has done to you. He is not the caring man he may have made himself out to be. His abuse has been seriously harmful to you. Let's be sure your feelings support your beliefs as well.

## EXERCISE: How Do You Feel Now About Your Partner's Control?

Throughout your recovery, especially when building inner resistance, you have been invited to pay attention to emerging feelings. We will once again do that here. This is a journaling exercise. With your journal, settle yourself in a quiet place.

When you're ready, think about your partner's degrading attacks: name-calling, hurtful put-downs, and scary and intimidating threats, as well as any physical harm he has done to you. From this place of remembering, focus on how you feel toward your partner. Recognize what feelings are emerging. Are any of them new? Take the time to sit with your feelings. This can help deepen the experience of your feelings, whatever they may be. When you're ready, journal about your feelings *toward* your partner, new and old, recurrent and occasional.

As you recognize your partner's behavior for what it is, it's not surprising if you find yourself feeling angry or if your anger is getting more intense at this point. In the recovery groups, some women begin by saying they feel irritated, annoyed, or frustrated with their partner and, in time, many feel it's okay to actually be more fully angry. Or you may have other negative feelings toward him such as disgust, loathing, or repulsion. Or you might feel sad and tearful about the horrific experiences he has put you through. All these feelings make sense, given his abuse of you.

It's when you can feel them that you're holding your partner responsible for his abuse. You also lessen the power of the distorted beliefs that supported you blaming yourself. This can reduce feelings of shame and guilt, and free you up to feel other feelings—including desires to take action and go after what you want.

If you feel angry or repulsed, there are a few ways to express your anger that are safe and beneficial to you. One way to get your feelings out is to write a letter to your partner that you'll never send. Express yourself to the fullest—say what you need to say and state it however you want—in order to lessen any bottled-up emotions. These are feelings that will not be acted on, nor expressed directly. Rather, they are a way to get at the depth of how you feel and get some relief. Another way to let your feelings out is to imagine expressing yourself. Recite to yourself what you would say if you could, in any way that feels satisfying. Or visualize taking some kind of action to express your feelings of anger or frustration. Expressing your negative feelings in safe ways can help lighten the burden by providing some relief for the painful feelings you've accumulated.

If you're having difficulty feeling anger or any negative feelings toward your partner for hurting you, or you feel numb and detached from your feelings, you might be blocked by negative beliefs you still hold about yourself. These negative beliefs are most likely the result of your partner's abusive coercion. Before we address those, let's first pay attention to getting back some positive beliefs you had about yourself before your relationship started.

When most women recall their lives prior to meeting their controlling partner, they report feeling more content, confident, and freer than they do now. Clearly, these women had beliefs about themselves that generated positive feelings at the time. Like them, you owe it to yourself to get back what you lost. To illustrate the next exercise, let's look at Marcy's experience of crying happy tears.

Marcy, a forty-year-old mother of two children, left her husband due to his abuse and unwillingness to make any changes. Throughout her fourteen-year marriage, she was often the recipient of degrading comments about her mothering—no matter what she did or didn't do. She struggled with feeling badly about herself as a mother, which caused her depression. For a positive belief exercise, Marcy relayed a wonderful moment when she heard her children sing a song they made up about her being the best mother ever. She felt deeply moved and realized that she is a good mother. It was a positive belief about herself that she lost sight of, since her soon-to-be ex-husband had often devalued her parenting. Marcy gradually got her self-worth and confidence back, which included the ways she parents her children.

EXERCISE: The Return to Positive Beliefs and Feelings

In recovery, some women have difficulty identifying something positive about themselves because their lives have been about abuse, hurt, and pain. With an abusive partner the positive beliefs about yourself, including strengths, that you felt before you ever met him become marginalized, or lost altogether. This exercise is about reconnecting with those parts of your self that hold positive beliefs. This is a journaling exercise, so when you're settled and feel ready, you can begin. There are two ways to approach this exercise; read through both and decide which one seems more doable for you.

Identify a time, before the abuse, when you felt positive, perhaps strong, capable, courageous, or smart—come up with your own adjectives that describe how you felt. For example, let's say you recall a time when you felt strong. From that place of strength within you, identify the positive beliefs and feelings that support this. Write them down. These positive beliefs are you; they are a reminder of who you are. If you'd like, you can use an image to represent this part of yourself. When you need to or want to, recall the image that can bring forth positive sensations. Do this exercise a number of times to uncover more positive beliefs. When you do, take in each belief and own it again.

Here's another way to approach this exercise. Think of three or more positive memories that occurred at any time in your life prior to your relationship. Write out a brief description of each positive experience and what you feel when recalling the memory. Then identify the positive belief you have about yourself now as a result of that positive experience. Give yourself time to fully take in the positive feelings about yourself that the belief holds. Do this for each memory you recall.

When we have positive experiences, beliefs and good feelings about ourselves emerge and help us feel better. Even recalling them later can bring forth the positivity again. This journal entry of positive beliefs is a place to return to when you need to be reminded or to lift your spirits. This list is a good reality check for you and a great defense when you experience negative attacks to your character, behavior, or feelings. Spend time reminding yourself of these beliefs so your self-esteem benefits and your confidence grows.

# Coercive Tactics Create Negative Beliefs

Individuals exposed to traumatic experiences, as I mentioned earlier, are often left with a distorted sense of themselves and the world around them. They can find themselves plagued by negativity, which shows up in the following ways (Shapiro 2001):

- Defectiveness beliefs such as, "It's my fault," "I'm not good enough," "There's something wrong with me."

- Safety and vulnerability beliefs such as, "I'm in danger," "I'm vulnerable."

- Power and control beliefs such as, "I'm powerless," "I have no control."

All three types of negative beliefs can develop from the coercive abuse you endured from your partner. In the next exercise, identify negative beliefs that you developed as a result of your partner's hurtful accusations that demeaned you, but are not true. Using self-observation, what negative beliefs do you hold about yourself that you did not have before the relationship began? You might notice negative beliefs you have as internalized self-critical messages to yourself that can play over and over in your head and make you feel terrible.

Let's return to Brenda, who you read about in chapter 6. She came to believe and value her husband's negative perspective of her as stupid and incompetent more than her own perspective. This was because she internalized his false accusations and they became negative beliefs about herself. Brenda benefitted when she revisited these beliefs and decided what was true for her, distinguished from what he distorted or made up to coerce her. When Brenda recognized her intelligence and capability, she denounced the negative belief, "I'm stupid." She came back to believing in herself again. Remember, she represented herself in court and won. You too can believe favorably in yourself again.

Your present self that has gradually been changing and getting stronger can get hijacked by the part of you that still holds old negative beliefs about yourself from your partner's abuse. Even though those beliefs may feel true, remind yourself constantly that they do not remain true today. Put them in the past—no longer do you need to believe them. Visualize putting them in a jar and burying the jar. Or write out the old beliefs on paper and set it on fire in a symbolic gesture of destroying them.

We can change negative beliefs into new positive beliefs. Find evidence to support the new belief. Jen's story from chapter 7 can help you see how negative beliefs can be reframed into positive beliefs that serve to strengthen you.

If you recall, Jen returned home from the park and found her husband enraged because she and the kids were not home and had not left a note. He cornered her in the kitchen and, while standing over her, raged on and on with his spit hitting her face. Jen might describe feeling anxious, scared, or even terrified. From this traumatic experience, her negative belief about herself might be, "I'm powerless"—and in that moment she *felt* powerless. This negative belief is about the lack of control.

If I asked her what positive belief could she feel now, Jen might say, "I have choices and can do something to protect myself." From this positive belief, she can feel empowered to help herself going forward. Or Jen might have had a different reaction. She might believe from his demeaning and blaming attacks that she had done something wrong—like not leaving a note. This negative belief speaks to her feelings of being defective and responsible for what happened to her. The belief could be, "I'm not good enough." Or, "I'm inadequate." The positive belief Jen might identify instead and come to feel is, "I'm okay and don't deserve to be treated this way."

As you see, negative beliefs have more to do with feelings. For example, one of Jen's beliefs, "I'm not good enough," means she is *feeling* that she's not good enough, but that doesn't mean it's true. This last point is most important to take to heart.

## EXERCISE: Recognize Negative Beliefs from His Hurtful Accusations

This is a journaling exercise, so have your journal available. Once you're settled in a quiet place, you can begin. Make a list of negative beliefs you currently hold about yourself. The following questions can help and can also prepare you for the later parts of the exercise. For each belief, ask yourself:

- When did the belief start?

- What ignited it?

- Did you have this belief before the relationship?

- Does any other part of your life support this belief?

Determine if the beliefs you identified line up with your partner's blaming and degrading accusations of you. Organize the negative beliefs into a column with the heading "Negative Beliefs from My Partner." This will give you a list of negative beliefs that resulted specifically from his harmful accusations and messages embedded in his coercive behavior. If you had any of the negative beliefs before you met your partner, and his abuse intensified them, that still doesn't mean that they are true for you. Add them to the list. If you still hold that they are true, then know they don't have to continue to be true any longer.

Now, create a second column next to the first, so that the beliefs line up. Label the column "Positive Beliefs About Myself." Look at the negative beliefs you listed and reframe them into positive beliefs about yourself. Do this for each negative belief you listed and fill in your column of newly desired positive beliefs.

When you're done, take stock of the information you gathered in the two columns. This is a powerful display of you taking back yourself. Keep working on taking in positive beliefs and strengthening yourself.

Negative beliefs about yourself that include, "I'm not safe," mean you don't feel safe and this needs to be taken seriously—whether your controlling partner is physically violent, threatens violence, or behaves in such a frightening or intimidating way that you fear for your safety. This also holds true if you've just left an abusive partner, which we'll address further in chapter 14. Evaluating your situation for physical safety first is always in your best interest. You can revisit Chapter 10 for help with safety planning. If you're recovering from a past abusive relationship, you might be physically safe at present but feel unsafe emotionally because you are plagued by old memories. Beyond the coping strategies mentioned in Chapter 7, those feelings are real and can be addressed in psychotherapy to help you heal and eventually feel safe.

We've been recapturing and building positive beliefs and tackling negative beliefs that resulted from your partner's abuse. In doing so, we've been lessening some of the related negative feelings such as shame, guilt, and anxiety. This recovery process will vary for different people. Some will follow the exercises, make changes, and feel some relief, while others might make changes but need more time and support to shift from negative beliefs and vulnerable feelings to relief. This is not your fault in any way, but something to keep in mind so you don't put undue pressure on yourself. Beyond the common experience of a controlling partner, we all have our own life experiences that uniquely impact the recovery process for each of us. Any change you've made is progress.

One negative feeling that can get in the way of recovery is fear, and that's because it's related to your personal safety. Changes in your negative beliefs are not instrumental in changing the emotional or physical danger caused by your partner's abuse but, most importantly, they help you feel stronger and able to take steps to protect yourself. Feeling physically and emotionally safe is necessary for your recovery, and a condition we should expect with our intimate partners. We'll revisit safety in chapter 14.

## You've Got This!

Controlling partners, through psychological abuse and brainwashing, cause traumatic changes in us that include negative beliefs and feelings, keeping us vulnerable. By recognizing and changing these beliefs, it's possible to allow positive feelings about ourselves to emerge or reemerge. To defend against your partner, positive beliefs and feelings are your shield and armor. They build self-esteem, confidence, and trust in your thinking and perception. Strong personal beliefs create the best resistance to brainwashing and a controlling partner's agenda.

# CHAPTER 13

# Empower Yourself— Take Back Your Life

Throughout your recovery, you've been weathering powerful and painful realizations about your relationship and, in particular, your partner. You identified the traumatic effects that you carry from your partner's coercion, which shows the depth of harm you have endured. In the last chapter, you addressed negative beliefs about yourself that resulted from your partner's abuse and countered those with positive alternatives. These were not only glimpses—you were creating room within yourself for positive beliefs and feelings to emerge. At a pace that works for you, you can use this momentum to actively take back who you are. This impressive feat says so much about you. Take it in and savor the positive beliefs and good feelings.

At this point in recovery, the question is often asked: what makes a successful relationship? I imagine that you are wondering about this also, so we start this chapter by looking at answers. Then, with your new insight, you'll revisit the goals you set in chapter 2 and recognize what you've accomplished so far. Finally, we'll address what you want and explore possible options with your partner.

## Successful Relationships

Research shows that when a partner dominates another through the abuse of power, it is a prime deterrent to a successful relationship (Greenberg and Goldman 2008). When a controlling partner uses coercive tactics to overpower you, it is a setup for the relationship to fail—without exception. Research about marital relationships in general reveals that husbands are likely to receive more support from their spouse and thus fair far better, while women tend to receive less support and experience greater stress from giving support. These are among the conditions that contribute to the higher rates of depression in women. All the stories I've shared so far, and your own experience with a controlling partner, stand as testimony to what doesn't work.

With an expanding body of research, we've learned that when a couple has equal or shared power in their relationship they are in the best position for success (Cooke 2006; Frisco and Williams 2003; Gottman and Silver 2000). To work toward an equal relationship, women (and their partners) need to pay attention to how they may have adapted to existing social and gender norms in relationships—even subconsciously. As a general rule, women's tendencies to be empathic and aware of the needs of others can be important strengths in relationships. However, this strong outward focus on another person can make it more difficult for women to articulate their own needs and ask directly for what they want (Jordan et al. 1991). To have a success-ful relationship, women need to be capable of focusing both outwardly and inwardly; being attuned to the needs of others while at the same time paying attention to their own needs *and* speaking up for what they want. When you make this a priority, your relationship has greater potential to succeed.

Since most women are widely positioned in the workforce and at the same time raising families, sharing domestic responsibilities with a partner has become all the more necessary. One study of couples believed to be successful at achieving work-family balance identified that having equality and a true partnership were the keys to success (Haddock and Bowling 2001).

What does an equal relationship look like? One significant study showed that when both partners see that they can influence the other person, they both have the experience of being heard and recognized. This mutual influence fosters open communication and the greater likelihood of sharing feelings, needs, and vulnerabilities. As a result, better intimacy is created in which both partners benefit and feel satis-fied with the relationship (Steil 1997).

However, as Gottman recognized in his long-term research on marriage, husbands were far less willing to be influenced and often stonewalled or distanced themselves verbally and emotionally from conversations (Gottman and Silver 2000). He also determined from his studies that 81 percent of men who are not willing to be influenced by their partner are at risk for divorce. That women seem more interested in a balanced relationship between partners might account for the findings that more women instigate divorce (Coontz 2005).

Western culture's patriarchal influence on social norms and practices has played an important role in creating these power differences between men and women. However, it's important for us to recognize that our social norms are created by what we do, which is social practice, and that makes norms open to change. This can be hugely empowering (Gergen 1999). Many individuals and couples have made a difference in their own lives, which illustrates that women (and men) can feel supported and satisfied in their relationships. Other findings suggest that equality in relationships, although not fully supported by many social institutions, is still progressing. Couples can forge a relationship of equal partnership when both partners have the desire, make the effort, and fully commit to making the relationship work for both.

With a controlling partner who needs to be in charge and dominate, you cannot have a successful relationship, or one that will benefit you, because you're left feeling invisible and unworthy. Ultimately, it's up to you and your partner to become aware of the influence of existing social norms that undermine the development of a relationship that benefits you both. Although it may not be perfectly equal, a conscious relationship can grow toward being more equal rather than less. Keep this idea of a relationship model that is known to be successful in mind as we turn to revisit your goals and address your concerns with your partner.

## Your Growth So Far

Before we look at your goals, let's pay tribute to all the work you have done so far to build internal resistance to your partner's abusive control and deconstruct your mindset that resulted from his coercion, which entrapped you. You've been slowly and steadily gaining knowledge and personal strength, and making whatever changes felt possible. As you learned about coercive tactics, you developed the ability to label your partner's behavior in real time—if you're still together. In doing so, you created a new perspective, with new beliefs, about his abuse. This allowed you to become more emotionally and cognitively removed in the moment, which helps lessen the hurtful impact of his accusations. Once you could see his behavior for what it is—psychological abuse—your confusion and self-doubt decreased as you built on this new insight into your relationship.

You also learned that your partner's abusive control impacted you, traumatically affecting your mental and physical health, which in turn made it harder to resist him. Previously, to minimize the abuse and risk of escalation, one of your defenses may have been to comply and, when you did, you had to suppress parts of yourself. But with new insight into previously held negative beliefs, such as blaming yourself for the abuse, you turned toward seeing that your partner is solely responsible. Addressing other negative beliefs helped you to reduce shame and guilt, making way for feelings like irritation or anger to emerge. When those feelings arise internally, by paying attention to them you now know what doesn't feel right —which can propel you toward being able to protect yourself.

As you build on positive beliefs within yourself and take back your strengths, more and more confidence builds. When you feel confident, you are in a position to trust your own judgment. What was one of your biggest losses before can now become your best self-protection going forward with your partner. Keep in mind that this recovery process takes time, so try not to pressure yourself to be done right away. Think of yourself as a work in progress. You're in a far better place now to keep healing and strengthening yourself than when you started.

After all you have learned and are now aware of, making a decision about your relationship is naturally a concern for you. First and foremost, you need to figure out what you want for yourself. With a controlling partner, this begins with adopting a new outlook and making room for yourself and what you want—that is your new priority. Whether or not you were good at this before meeting your partner, now is the time to make sure you pay attention to your needs and what is best for you—so you can take steps to get it.

## EXERCISE: Revisit Your Goals

At the beginning of your recovery in chapter 3, you created goals for yourself. You declared what you want to change, and confided your hopes and desires for the future. At this point, it's useful to look back at those goals to see your progress and what you have achieved thus far. Let's revisit the common themes for goals frequently cited by women in recovery. I'm imagining your goals might echo some or all of these.

Become clear about what exactly is happening in my relationship by learning about controlling behaviors, their impact, and how to best respond.

Become emotionally stronger by moving out of confusion to trust how I think, feel, and see things.

Feel like myself again by taking back those parts of myself that I lost trust in or had to keep hidden.

Meeting goals can be messy and not straightforward. From all my years of working with women in recovery, I have observed that it's unlikely that you will meet all your goals at this point. Women who are proud of their accomplishments focus on their growth so far and see the unfinished work as a series of goals to keep working toward with their new found wisdom.

In this spirit, turn to the goals you recorded in your journal. Read through them, giving careful thought to each. Write about what you have changed and achieved. Feel good about your changes and honor your hard work. Identify the positive belief that accompanies this moment. It could be "I have choices" or "I can make changes" or "I have control." These positive beliefs can be empowering. Next, identify what you're still working on and what you still want for your-self. This gives you focus and purpose to keep moving forward with healing and strengthening yourself.

## Decide What to Do About Your Relationship

Now is the time to figure out what you want to do about your relation-ship. At this point, the following three options come up for women in recovery. You'll see "working on getting stronger" is mentioned in each, because your healing will continue to be an important priority.

- Keep working on healing and getting stronger, learn more about controlling relationships, and decide not to make a decision about my relationship now. I need to give myself more time to figure it out.

- Keep working on getting stronger as I stay with my partner and ask him to change his behavior to make the relationship work for both of us.

- Keep working on getting stronger as I am clear I want to make a plan to leave safely because at least one of the following is true: I cannot be safe in my relationship, I've lost the desire to be in the relationship, or I've lost love for my partner.

With your new insights, if you've determined that you can't stay with your partner, then leaving in a planned and safe way is best. If your partner is also the father of your children, it's most likely that you'll need to keep co-parenting—so it can be very useful to continue to gain clarity about how to respond to his coercive behaviors. Both of these will be addressed in the next chapter.

If your choice is to stay with your partner, but wish to have a better relationship, then you need to figure out if your partner is willing to change. Here are some questions to think about:

- Can he give up his control and change beliefs that support him having power over you in the relationship?

- Can he truly take full ownership of and responsibility for his abusive behavior?

- Does he have the capacity to feel or develop empathy for you and the pain he has caused you (and your children)?

- Can he work with you to create a relationship that benefits you both?

- Does he have the desire to change?

In the recovery groups, women often ask how it's possible to know if they are with someone who can change. It comes down to whether he has the desire to change. Although the scenario by which a controlling partner changes is quite complex, I lead with a simple suggestion as a place to start: ask him to listen to your concerns. From your new place of insight and growth, you have an opportunity to speak about your relationship with your partner. If he's willing to be open to what you have to say, he will not do what he usually does, but will begin to listen. Then you can assess how long he will listen and whether he will actually work with you on the relationship.

The most critical factor for any changes to take place is whether or not he takes responsibility for his control and abuse. If he's not open to what you have to say, he'll react in the abusive and possibly escalating way that you have often experienced with him. What he is telling you quite emphatically is: "No!" This response informs you that your partner is not willing to listen to your feelings or take your concerns into consideration. It might even let you know that speaking about them is hurtful or even dangerous.

From decades of experience working with abusive men, Lundy Bancroft (2002) has recognized that it's unlikely for most abusers to change. Your controlling partner has a lot to give up and will not do so easily. He gets many rewards from his self-centeredness and his power over you. Usually, the only way he will change is when he is given no other choice. This requires you to show him that you can, and will, live without him—unless he changes. Bancroft suggests the following for what he calls "creating a context for change."

- Establish consequences for his abuse, if it continues. You would leave him, which requires advance preparation and a way to do so safely. It could involve the legal system if he becomes threatening, or physically or sexually violent.

- Make it very clear to him how you expect him to treat you by being specific about what you'll live with and what you will not live with.

- Keep working on your own healing and strengthening. He'll see your strength and know that, if he doesn't change, you're prepared to move on without him.

Your partner needs to commit to work on changing himself. This is tricky because, as you learned, he believes he's right and makes his needs more important than yours. His attitudes and expectations come out of these beliefs. Bancroft points out that abusive men who have been able to make lasting changes were able to realize the harm and pain they were causing their partner and children. They were able to learn "to care about what is good for others in the family and develop empathy, instead of caring only for themselves" (Bancroft 2002, 361). This is not easy for an abusive man to do and it will also not happen quickly. If he is successful, it may require a long period of receiving the right help and working on change.

Some women in the recovery groups have engaged in a trial separation to create an impetus for their partners to change. This gave their partners the clear message that they will not keep living the same way, nor will their children be exposed to coercive behavior or abuse any longer. During the separation, the partners who strongly wished to be with their spouse and family were motivated and sought help in a well-established treatment program for abusive men. These men needed to believe, and rightly so, that if they made the necessary changes and no longer used coercion, then they could get back together with their partners.

Getting a partner to agree to a separation can be quite difficult, but some women succeed with help from the legal establishment. Melanie was one woman who tried this with her husband of eighteen years. After a violent episode during which he destroyed personal property belonging to their fifteen-year-old son, she obtained a protective order for the first time—which brought everything to a head, including putting in place a separation. Here is her story.

*During the year of our separation, my husband regularly attended a program for abusive men which took up most of that year. We did not have much personal contact because I felt too vulnerable to what he might say or do and was afraid it would affect my commitment to stay separated. I did agree to get back together at the end of the year, if I felt he made the necessary changes.*

*While separated, I accepted his request to meet monthly with him and our rabbi. At these times, I would hear about the work he was doing and the changes he felt he was making. At the end of the year, we came together to review his progress with the counselor from his program. I heard that my husband had fulfilled the attendance requirement that the judge ordered. In fact, he had not missed one session and was clearly expecting to return home. But I also learned from his counselor that he had not made any significant changes in his attitudes, which would ensure that he interacts respectfully and that we would be safe. My husband left me with no choice but to divorce him.*

Because your relationship has been all about him, I want to be sure that you're taking the time to focus on and figure out, from deep in your heart, what you want for yourself, your family, and your future. Gradually this might have become clear or you still may not know.

## EXERCISE: What Do You Want?

This is a journaling exercise. Settle in somewhere comfortable, where you will have no interruptions and all the time you need. When you're ready, ask yourself the following questions and respond honestly—for yourself. Remember this is only for you to see and know.

- What do you want in a relationship?

- What does this desired relationship look like?

- If you were to get this relationship, what does it feel like to be in it?

- What would you experience?

- How would you feel about yourself?

- Can you have what you want for yourself (and your children) with your partner?

Take time to answer the last question—think about what you feel and truly believe. From your gut feeling, see whether what you want might be possible, or might not be possible, with your partner. You have a lot of information and more self-awareness at this point. If it helps, you can create two headings, one for what might make it possible and another for what might not make it possible. Then give the reasons for believing what you do and list them under the headings. You could even create a third heading for what you're not willing to compromise on—your bottom line items.

Your responses in this exercise can help you get clear enough to make a decision about your relationship. It might require more than one pass through, which is okay. In the next chapter, you'll find guided steps you can take for any decision you make as you determine what's possible.

## You've Got This!

Recognizing the ingredients of a successful relationship provides a backdrop for you to seriously consider what you want. Your goals tell you what you desire for yourself and your progress is the strength you've built within yourself to help you get there. Making room for what you want is a new priority. Keep strengthening this part of you, for it is this part that will help you to know what to do going forward.

CHAPTER 14

# Moving Forward—What Do You Want?

Here we are, at the last chapter of this book, although not at the end of your personal work in progress. You have moved out of denying and minimizing to clearly seeing the coercion in your partner's behavior. It's eye-opening to see this powerful influence that impacts intimate relationships and causes negative health issues and disempowering effects. What you want instead is a balanced, or more balanced, relationship in which both partners share influence and respect for each other. To strive for that, you need to be fully present to be yourself with your intimate partner—which gives you a chance to be at your best. Going forward, I hope you'll prioritize this for yourself, whether it's the relationship you're in or your relationships in the future.

Even as you have reason to feel good about your newfound awareness and growing strength, your recovery is still ongoing. Now it's time to decide what you want for yourself and understand what it means for your relationship. In this chapter, we'll cover: responses to coercive tactics that show your new expectations for the relationship going forward; the decision to stay with a controlling partner who might change; the decision to leave a controlling partner who will not change—and how to do so safely; how to co-parent with a controlling partner after divorce; and how to continue recovery in every case. Keep in mind that all decisions are yours to make. Whether your partner's control is mild, moderate, or severe, I truly believe that you know your situation best and can decide accordingly.

At this point, ask yourself if you still care about and love your partner enough to even try to mend the relationship. With increasing trust in your thinking and judgment, you are more adept at knowing what you want for yourself.

## First Know Your Legal Rights

If you're married, clarifying your legal rights might be necessary before you can decide what to do about your relationship. Women in recovery often have incorrect information about what to expect if they were to leave their spouse. Usually the misinformation is the result of a controlling partner's threats and other menacing messages that were said to coerce and frighten, such as, "If you leave, you'll be leaving without your children" or "I'll see to it that you never get the kids" or "You'll have no money and be living out of your car." Threats of this type are often unfounded, but without clarification they can result in women feeling trapped and without options—when in fact, they have options. The best way to get clear is to obtain up-to-date, accurate information about your legal rights by contacting a local domestic violence organization or meeting with a divorce lawyer who has experience working with clients in abusive relationships.

If you meet with a lawyer, it's not necessary to have reached a decision regarding your relationship. It's a chance to learn about your rights, review your fears and safety options, and know what to expect if you were to leave. In addition, you can learn about your local state laws and what is financially customary in a divorce—including child support and alimony, custody, co-parenting plans that include visitation and communication, and any other issues of concern. If your history with your partner includes threats of harm or physical or sexual violence, you will also learn about your choices for legal protection. As you contemplate what to do, having correct information about your legal rights and options for protection helps you make the best decision for yourself and your children.

## Building a Life Without Coercion

You have a new lens for looking at yourself, your partner, and your relationship, so you might feel ready to build a new life without abuse. From this place of strength, you might feel ready to conduct yourself differently and make it known to your partner what you now expect. Your experience with your partner gives you the best information for what might be possible going forward in the relationship and what to watch out for. If you feel it's necessary, safety planning is an option to put in place first. If you believe it's not safe to speak with your partner directly about his coercive behavior, or to change your behavior in ways that demonstrate your expectations going forward, then it's best not to do so. Later in the chapter, I'll share safer ways to approach your partner to create a scenario for change or to leave.

There are guidelines that can help you make different choices for responding to coercive tactics that your partner uses. Your reactions to his behaviors need to reflect your new expectations for yourself and the relationship you're striving to have. If your partner is willing to respect your new boundaries and the limits you're setting, he'll work to change his behavior and you will begin to see that he's taking you seriously. If he resorts to abuse, he's letting you know that he's not taking you seriously or that he needs to work on himself first, before he's ready to work with you on the relationship. I'll address treatment options for abusive men shortly. Here are guidelines for responding to coercive behaviors.

## Isolation

Your partner needs to respectfully support you as an independent adult. Let your partner know that you need to see your family or friends from time to time, and to come and go without answering to him. He needs to trust you, especially if you haven't given him real reasons— not imagined ones—not to trust you. He'll need to manage his feelings about this change and his trust issue—this is his problem to work on. If he still doesn't tolerate you having contact with others, this can inform your decision about staying with him or not.

## Monopolization of Perception

When he responds to you by lying, scrutinizing your thinking, distorting the meaning of your words, twisting the truth, or blaming you—all aimed to misdirect you—determine what you believe to be true and hold firm to that. If you wish to speak up, don't tell him he's lying, for example, just tell him you have a different perspective and don't agree with him. Or tell him that you recall what happened differently and that you trust your own recollection. If he distorts the truth to make you responsible, you can declare that you know you're not and won't take responsibility.

Can he tolerate the fact that you hold a different view? You could even venture to point out what you observe about his behavior that makes communication with him impossible. Decide not to listen or engage with him in this type of exchange. In the end, holding to your own beliefs is a position of strength and lets you see how he chooses to respond. At the same time, it will feel empowering for you.

Another way monopolization of perception can be used is when you approach him with a concern directly. If you bring up your issue and he counters with a defensive attack about you or about something completely different, let him know right away that you can discuss his concern later—for right now you need him to stay with your topic. Then restate your concern. If he again goes on an attack, let him know that if he's not willing to discuss your issue, you'll need to end the conversation. If it happens again, let him know that you're done talking and then separate yourself. The more you can do this consistently for yourself, the better you will feel. Some partners, in time, stop defensive attacking and start paying attention. By staying grounded in your position, you're standing up for you, but also allowing him to evolve—if he can.

## Devaluation and Humiliation

When you hear put-downs, name calling, or degrading statements of any kind directed toward you, don't defend yourself by responding to the content of his attacks. This will only feed his stance. Instead *address his behavior*—what he's doing. Let your partner know that, if he doesn't stop putting you down or if he keeps talking to you in this way, you'll need to end the conversation. At some point, if you choose to respond directly, counter with something like, "You telling me I'm stupid doesn't make me stupid" or "You telling me I'm a bad mother doesn't make me a bad mother." This has the benefit of reinforcing your belief that, in the case of the latter example, you're a good mother and are showing him that he cannot take this away from you. Again, see how he handles you having your own perspective and voice.

## Demonstrating Omnipotence or Superiority

Your controlling partner's attitude that he's superior to you does not mean that he is superior, nor do you need to go along with his erroneous belief. You get to decide how you see yourself in relation to him. When he enforces trivial demands like telling you what to do, for example, you can simply say, "No." You don't need to offer an explanation that he can then pick apart—instead offer an explanation only if he can accept it.

The point is that you're an adult and free to choose. If you are willing to do something he's asking of you, but don't like the way he's approaching you, you can say, "I need you to ask me in another way" or "I need you to ask me in a way that's more respectful." You determine your own expectations for your relationship, such as how you'd like to share domestic responsibilities and childrearing, and then negotiate. You need to feel respected for what you bring to the relationship and family. It's up to him whether he can work toward meeting you at least halfway.

## Occasional Indulgences

When he's trying to get back in your good graces after being abusive and move you into ignoring what just happened, your best response is to hold him responsible for what he did and the hurt he caused you. Tell him how you feel about what he did. Let him know that you need for him to recognize and own his abusive behavior. If he can't, he's letting you know that the relationship has no chance of changing. If he attempts to get you to share the blame by pointing out what you said or did, tell him it's unacceptable to blame you. You can take ownership for what you said or did that upset him and offer to discuss it, but you have no responsibility for his abusive reaction. He has many other choices. If he attempts to play on your sympathy and get you to feel sorry for him because of his issues, let him know that if he believes he behaves badly because of his issues then he needs to get himself help. It does not give him a pass for hurting you. Let him know that when he's ready to take responsibility and be sincere about his abuse, you'll be willing to hear what he has to say.

### Threats

All threats are unacceptable, whether it has to do with turning off your credit card, abandoning you, or physically harming you. Threats are meant to coerce, restrict your life, and make you unsafe. When you hear a threat of any kind, you can tell your partner this: "That's a threat. You can't threaten me if you expect to have a relationship with me." Be consistent with addressing his threats. If he doesn't show you that he's taking you seriously, then you'll likely know what you need to do.

### Induced Debility and Exhaustion

Your partner's abuse and coercion may have caused a decline in your mental and physical health. You've been working on your recovery and learning strategies to create a safer life for yourself (and your children) either with your partner or without. Your safety is most critical to a full recovery, so keep prioritizing it.

The more you can remain strong and consistent in your expectations and responses to your partner, the more you'll be able to tell by his reactions what might be possible. If you're still interested in him, this experience can help you decide, eventually, whether to stay or leave.

## Approaching Your Partner About His Control

If you feel it's unsafe to approach your partner, or you have learned that when you try the above strategies your partner becomes abusive, then your two choices are to create a scenario that could possibly bring about change and see what he does, or to make a plan to leave safely. Characteristics of a controlling partner that indicate a higher risk of danger are essential to take into consideration, such as a partner who is physically and sexually violent and uses threats of harm. If this describes your partner and you'd like to speak to him, it is not a good idea to do it alone. With the help of a domestic violence advocate, you can create a "context of change" for a partner with a thought-out plan. This plan can: make your situation as safe as possible; express your desire to remain in the relationship with him; and at the same time let him know that, if he doesn't give up his abusive control, you're prepared to move on without him. Include the following helpful elements.

- Decide on a place to have the conversation that allows you to leave quickly.

- Select a setting that doesn't contain items that can be used against you.

- Identify the behaviors that your partner exhibits just before he resorts to physical violence. Use this as the time, *before* the violent eruption, to leave quickly.

- Know where your car is, have access to your keys, and reconcile within yourself that you may need to call the police for help.

- Have a trusted person present who doesn't deny or minimize your partner's abuse, supports you, and also wants him to get help.

- Arrange in advance to send a text to another person, perhaps a friend, so he or she can call the police for help if necessary.

Giving your partner an ultimatum that you're fully prepared to follow through on is taking a position of strength and provides evidence of what might be possible with your partner.

If your partner hasn't been violent or has never threatened violence and you wish to speak with him about his coercive behavior, keep in mind that he could still escalate and become violent. Although you might feel it's less necessary, safety planning in a situation like this can be useful as well. When Janet, a thirty-three-year-old married woman, decided to approach her partner of six years about his psychological abuse, she devised a creative plan using a baby monitor. Her neighbor listened to the conversation just in case she needed help (although it turned out she did not).

# Navigating Treatment

If you feel it's time to raise your concerns and you're ready to do so, be prepared to make your expectations for his behavior change clear and give consequences for abusive behavior—which ultimately includes leaving if he doesn't change. You need to know that controlling partners do not change on their own and without appropriate help. If you hear, "Okay, I'll change," this is not acceptable; nor is it what you're looking for. To increase the likelihood that he can succeed in changing, your partner would benefit the most by participating in a reputable treatment program for abusive men. Since we know that controlling partners believe they are not responsible for their actions and often distort the truth, a good treatment program or an individual therapist specialized in working with abusive men will also speak to you periodically about your experience with him. If your partner accepts help with this communication in place, it's a step in the right direction and places him in the best position to be helped. Then it's a matter of him working hard to take full advantage of the help. At this point, a treatment program for abusive men is far better than individual treatment.

You might hear from your partner that he'd be willing to do couples therapy instead, or you could be wondering about this yourself. Couples therapy is often a form of treatment that controlling partners will try first because if they enter treatment alone, it's inferred that they have a problem and that's usually intolerable at the outset. As you have learned, most controlling partners do not take responsibility for their behavior but blame you instead. That's why entering treatment with you can allow him to continue to believe you're the problem. In couples therapy he's apt to dominate the session, or at least try, to suit his agenda—which can come out of a distorted reality. Given that you're afraid of speaking up to your partner, or in front of your partner, you very likely won't feel safe enough to state your concerns directly or disagree with him wholeheartedly. If you do, you risk payback later in the form of abuse outside the session. In the end, the couples therapist will hear more of his concerns, which leads to a mistaken view of you and your relationship.

After hearing too many frustrating and failed attempts at couples therapy, I find myself not recommending it as a first step for getting help, especially when there is a history of physical or sexual violence and threats of harm. Shelly's experience highlights some themes that I hear over and over again.

Shelly, together with her psychologically abusive husband of nine years, saw a couples therapist. After a year of participating and feeling frustrated and unhelped, she ended the therapy and sought a divorce. She then decided to contact the couples therapist to meet individually for one session. Shelly asked, "Why did you support my husband's demand to have sex every other day?" The therapist told her that she was concerned he wouldn't stay in treatment otherwise. She then told Shelly that her husband was so unreasonable that it was great Shelly finally reached the decision to divorce him on her own.

These are the two problematic issues with couples treatment. First, the therapist accommodates the controlling partner in some way to keep him in treatment for the benefit of the couple's work—while fueling the self-righteousness that plays out at home. Then, because of the therapist's accommodation, the woman is called upon to also "accommodate," causing her to feel confused, unheard, and unsupported—the very same experience she has with her partner outside of therapy.

If you're inclined to go this route, your bottom line should be for the couples therapist to be well-trained in working with individuals who are psychologically abusive and, if this is the case, physically violent against their intimate partner. Also, a good couples therapist will conduct an individual session with each partner after the first or second joint session. This allows you to express concerns, disclose the abuse, and ask questions that otherwise may not get verbalized. Sometimes, this practice of meeting individually results in a natural weeding out of controlling partners who won't tolerate their spouse or girlfriend being seen alone. In order to create a safe setting, it's also important for the couples therapist to keep confidential what they hear during the individual sessions unless given permission to share. Once this occurs as part of evaluating a couple, with this information the therapist can determine the best overall treatment approach for the couple going forward.

One approach that has proven useful for relationships with controlling partners is for each member of the couple to initially participate in treatment focused on themselves. Coercive men can be referred to a specialized treatment program and women referred to individual or group therapy addressing controlling relationships, trauma recovery, and self-esteem. Eventually, they can come together to work in couples therapy when he can listen, be respectful, and take responsibility for his behavior, and when she is no longer afraid, feels confident, and can speak up for herself. Ultimately, a controlling partner's best chance to improve is to enter specialized treatment for abusive men, however he might get there. Expect no less if you're serious about a life with him without coercion and abuse.

## Leaving Your Controlling Partner

If you realize that you can't create a safe relationship with your partner—because he's too dangerous for you to approach, or you have tried without success, or he refuses to get help, or you just don't have it in you to be with him anymore—then leaving is your best option. But because it presents a serious threat to his power and control, this time can be the most dangerous, especially when there's a history of threats, and physical or sexual violence. If you believe you could be in imminent harm when you leave, then speak with a domestic violence advocate to learn options for staying safe. Take whatever time you can to carefully plan your departure and contact organizations that can help you, which are offered in the Resources section in this book.

This period of transition is an emotionally challenging time. You're leaving the person you had hoped to share your life with, perhaps raise your family with, and maybe even grow old with. In addition to the fear of your partner's reaction to your leaving, you can experience sadness and grief over the loss of the relationship and possibly an increase in anxiety and depression for a period of time. Keep in mind that feeling worse is temporary and doesn't mean your decision to leave is wrong. Also, don't give up your plan to leave because the feelings seem unbearable. Given how emotionally challenging this transition can be, you might consider getting emotional support from a psychotherapist, a group focused on leaving an abusive relationship, an informed counseling program in your religious community, or friends with whom you can regularly communicate. During this transition, be sure to take care of yourself the best you can.

If your partner hasn't been physically or sexually violent and has not threatened harm, it's unlikely you'll be able to get a protective order. If you don't have children together, you are freer to leave and plan accordingly. If you're married and have children, it can be challenging to physically separate from a controlling partner without a protective order. Most controlling partners will not willingly walk out of the house at your request. And it's not a good idea for you to leave the family home with your children in an attempt to separate. Speak with a divorce attorney about your situation so they can help you determine your options, including getting a vacate order.

After the relationship ends, most controlling partners will work hard to seduce their girlfriends or spouses back. You're likely to hear familiar promises to change or get help. The positive behaviors you experience during Phase 3 of the abuse cycle are likely to show up and can bring back feeling hopeful and make you consider reconciling. If you feel vulnerable to being coerced by your ex-partner or you feel yourself weakening in response to his promises, it's a good time to ground yourself by revisiting your "Controlling Behavior Checklist" and reading through your journal to bring to mind his abuse and all the reasons you left.

To protect yourself, let him know in advance not to call or contact you. Then be consistent in not taking his calls and not responding to e-mails or texts so there is no risk of giving him a mixed message. Be prepared to block his phone number through your cell phone provider or phone company.

The best way women can successfully leave a controlling partner and move on is to not let their ex-partner have access to them. The exception is when children are involved.

## Challenges of Co-Parenting After the Relationship Ends

If you're leaving or have left your controlling partner, yet need to have him in your life because you have children together, be thoughtful about the ways you choose to communicate going forward. Don't expect that your partner's style of communicating after divorce will change because he is out of the relationship. Many women quickly learn that his way of communicating remains the same and, in fact, can get worse. Your leaving—the ultimate threat to his power and control—can cause anger and resentment that lingers long after you have departed.

One fifty-two-year-old woman divorced her husband but periodically had contact with him because of their three children. On one occasion, her youngest, a girl in high school, needed a passport for a class trip, which required both parents to be together at a post office to sign documents. Her brief encounter with him was tense and stressful, culminating in his refusal to pay for half the cost—something their divorce agreement required. As she was leaving the post office, she overheard an employee say to her ex-husband, "Someday I hope you can love your daughter as much as you hate your ex-wife."

Here lies the problem for many women who divorce controlling partners. Their ex-partner can continue to give them a hard time through their only means of contact—the co-parenting arena. What's best for the children can become secondary as his fierce retribution toward his ex-wife takes front and center. When these episodes happen, it's stressful for the mother and hurtful to the children. Sometimes, a third person such as a parenting coordinator can be an option to help with parenting issues. Divorce attorneys can provide information about this type of support.

When you divorce with children, make sure you have planned out the type of contact that works best for you and be sure it's detailed and included in your divorce agreement. The best arrangement is to limit contact to e-mails for issues regarding the children only. Plan to use this arrangement for a long period of time. While texting might be necessary in situations when the other parent needs to be informed right away, e-mail gives you a paper trail if you should need to show that your ex-partner is threatening, harassing, or not co-parenting in the best interest of the children. It also gives you time to be thoughtful about how you'd like to respond. Use the responses to coercive tactics suggested earlier in this chapter, if necessary. Your growing strength and trust in your own judgment will help you set limits and keep clear boundaries when advocating for your children's needs and interests.

In the Resources section, you'll find websites that divorced parents can use to communicate and that will provide a record of e-mails, if needed. Domestic violence advocates and some divorce attorneys can suggest guidelines to put in place for communicating during a separation or divorce.

## When Does Recovery End?

Although recovery varies for each woman, there are some general considerations that impact everyone. In many cases, symptoms subside once you're not being coerced and abused because he has truly changed and you're no longer feeling at risk, or he is no longer in your life. Simply put, your recovery is likely to be complete when you're *safe*, physically and emotionally. This is when you are able to be you—freely acting and expressing yourself without fear of reprisal. You can trust your perception and determine what you need and want.

When these conditions are not yet met or are not enough for you to feel safe in your body, you can benefit from additional support. The paragraphs that follow each describe scenarios with various levels of safety, depending on your circumstances.

You're not feeling ready to make your new expectations known, so you use the tools you've learned to protect yourself—internally—to minimize the impact of your partner's coercion. With safety measures in place and with the benefits you receive from individual or group therapy for additional emotional support, you can shore up your growth until you feel able to make a decision and take steps accordingly.

You're standing up for yourself more with your partner, making your expectations known, and you have safety options in place in case you need them. You're not feeling completely safe, but are working at getting there and sensing progress. At some point you'll know if you can stay, or want to stay, with your partner. If not, you know that leaving him will be the only way to be fully safe and free to have the life you want.

You've set an ultimatum, a context for change with the hope your partner will accept treatment for abusive men—or you'll need to leave him. While he's working on himself, a temporary separation gives you a chance to feel safer. If he supports your need to do this for yourself, he's moving in the right direction. The other option is not to separate, but he's showing a commitment to treatment by following through. In the meantime, you've made your expectations for his behavior clear. Ultimately, if he can change and sustain it over time, you will eventually feel emotionally and physically safe with him.

You now know that leaving is your only option and you've put in place the best plan to do so as safely as possible with the help of others. After a while, with your partner completely out of your life and without contact for a period of time, you return to feeling safe. When you do, parts of yourself re-emerge—thoughts, feelings, and strengths you had prior to the relationship. You'll have a chance to feel like yourself again.

You have left your abusive partner and no longer have any contact but your trauma symptoms continue through flashbacks, distressing memories or dreams, bodily sensations, depression, or other symptoms that you indicated on the checklist in chapter 11. These symptoms prevent you from feeling emotionally safe and moving on with your life. This is a sign that further attention to healing is necessary. It's in your best interest to seek psychotherapy with a clinician who understands trauma and controlling partners.

You left your partner but continue to have contact through co-parenting your children. You have your own recovery to work on and can tell, for example, when you feel scared just by receiving his e-mail. This is an ideal time to get additional support to help you heal, navigate this new form of communicating, and strongly support your children's agenda.

You have untreated trauma that occurred prior to meeting your partner, which was further compounded by your partner's abuse. You can attend to this trauma as well so that, with the right therapeutic help, your healing can help you cope and feel safe. The Resources section has suggestions under the heading "Mental Health and Trauma Treatment."

As you can see, to be ourselves and function at our best, it's necessary to feel safe. So keep working toward this goal for yourself and make it a required condition in your relationships.

## Your Life Going Forward

Although you're coming to the end of this particular process in your recovery, your self-care continues throughout your life. For now, there are some considerations to be aware of and address, if they apply to you.

- Many women feel deep shame for loving a person who hurt them so much. Recognize the power of not knowing or seeing, and have compassion for yourself.

- There is a high use of alcohol for women with controlling partners. If this is true for you, consider AA or SMART recovery groups for help and support. Without this type of recovery, a controlling partner can use this against you in a divorce to influence the issue of custody of your children. Protect yourself first.

- Make a commitment to take care of your body and spirit by doing good things for your self like meditation or yoga. Yoga has proven to be helpful with trauma recovery.

- Learn ways to feel and express your anger so you can respectfully speak up for yourself and assert your self by setting limits and having clear boundaries.

- Be sure to stay connected with others who care about you— friends, family, co-workers—or by pursuing new friendships.

- No matter how difficult things get or how upset you feel, make a commitment to yourself to not criticize your husband or ex-husband to your children, for he is their father. Children want to love and be loved by both parents. Venting your feelings can give you relief, but be sure you do it in other ways.

- If you're worried about your children, an evaluation by a guidance counselor at their school or child therapist can determine if they need support and, if so, what would be most helpful.

- When you need to, return to your journal or this book to review what you learned and to get back on track.

If you're thinking ahead, it's possible you're having thoughts about a new relationship at some time in your future. After ending their relationship, many women can't imagine dating at all or dating any time soon. It's common to have trust issues and be fearful of being hurt again. With time and recovery, these issues usually do lessen. What you have going for you is a deep understanding of coercive tactics and personal knowledge of what it feels like when you're the recipient of such tactics. With this awareness, the ability to stand up for yourself, and by knowing what you want in an intimate relationship, you're in a much better position to recognize and avoid controlling partners and succeed in finding a caring and compatible partner to not lose your life to, but to truly share your life with.

The following affirmations were created by a group of women toward the end of their recovery. These words came from clear minds and strong hearts—I hope they inspire you.

- I am not responsible for my partner's behavior.

- I have the right to be an equal partner in this relationship.

- I have a right to be angry when I am mistreated.

- I have a right to express my anger in a productive way.

- I have the right to be treated with respect.

## You've Got This!

Arriving at yourself—or taking yourself back—has been a journey and one I hope you continue with earnest. You are the only one who knows what's best for you: what you need, want, like, and don't like. Be the director of your own life. When you feel there's some negative influence coming your way, trust your gut—you'll know what doesn't feel right or feels unfair. Set your limits and keep your boundaries. As you go forward with life and relationships, always be sure to honor your own strong beliefs and innermost desires for yourself. I wish you well.

# Acknowledgments

During the many years I have been writing this book, I have amassed people to thank—some easily identifiable and others who, while unnamed, have had an enduring influence on my persevering all this time.

I'm forever grateful to Hadley Fisk, MSW, my friend, colleague, and cofounder of the groups for women with controlling partners. So many years ago, Hadley courageously and creatively ventured with me into a new realm of clinical interest—domestic violence—and together we grew passion for this deeply gratifying work.

I'm tremendously thankful to the committed women who formed The Network for Women's Lives, an organization designed to eradicate domestic violence and that enthusiastically provided the supportive arena for launching our recovery groups. The Network's subsidy, which made it possible for all women to attend, has since continued through the committed work of the Domestic Violence Services Network.

In my approach to trauma and the way I engage those I wish to help, I deeply appreciate the clinical training and keen influence from many mentors and colleagues and, in particular, wish to thank Debbie Korn, PhD.

In the process of writing this book, I'm thankful first and foremost to Lisa Tener, my writing coach and book proposal editor of many years, who patiently supported me as this book alternately took front and center in my life, and then receded, only to rebound. Her sincere encouragement to get my topic out there and her belief in me—that I could write and find a publisher—leave me eternally grateful. I'm deeply appreciative of Stuart Horwitz, book coach and editor, who jumped in with quick readiness to give thoughtful input in bringing

the final book to life. At the very beginning, Cynthia Shearer guided
me in my early ideas of the book. I'm grateful for her thoughtful direction that started me on this path.

As for the committed people at New Harbinger, I'm deeply grateful to Catharine Meyers, who embraced my book proposal and believed
in the book it could become, and to Vicraj Gill, whose comments
clarified and improved early chapters. I also wish to thank Jennifer
Holder for her careful editing.

Many family members and friends showed heartfelt interest and
support along the way. My mother-in-law Joan Robart will sadly not
see this publication, but I will always be grateful for her unwavering
support. To the many wonderful friends who supported and encouraged me—I thank them all. To one friend in particular, Abby Adis, I
deeply appreciate her attention to the reader's feelings during their
recovery, to which she offered thoughtful input. My loving family,
Alison, Cory, and daughter-in-law Kathleen, I'm forever grateful for
your encouragement and for being in my life.

Most importantly, I'm eternally thankful to all the women who
courageously made their way to the recovery groups. Your stories, your
commitment, and your transformations to create better lives for your-
selves and your families are truly remarkable. I deeply appreciate how
your growth inspires me.

# Resources

## Domestic Violence and Psychological Abuse

### The National Domestic Violence Hotline

1-800-799-SAFE (7233), http://www.thehotline.org

- Offers safety planning—all calls are confidential

- For women, men, LGBTQ people, and all cultures

- Trained, expert advocates are available 24–7 and speak 170 languages

- Provides referrals to local helplines, resources, and support groups

- Access online information about safety planning by clicking on the Get Help tab and selecting "Path to Safety" from the drop-down menu

- Access their list of recommended reading by clicking on the Resources tab, then the Publications tab

- Blog entry for advice on finding the right therapist: http://www.thehotline.org/2013/07/finding-the-right-counselor-for-you/

- Information on treatment programs for abusive behavior http://www.thehotline.org/2014/07/intervention-programs-for-abusive-behavior/

### National Center on Domestic Violence, Trauma, and Mental Health

http://www.nationalcenterdvtraumamh.org

**National Coalition Against Domestic Violence**

http://www.ncadv.org/need-help/get-help

- Help with safety planning, including a list of questions that can help you create your own personalized plan

- Provides legal assistance, including questions to ask before you hire a lawyer

**National Network to End Domestic Violence**

http://www.nnedv.org

**WomensLaw.org**

http://www.womenslaw.org

- Find local legal help and other local resources for domestic violence

- Child custody information

# Books on Abuse and Violence

Bancroft, Lundy and Jac Patrissi. *Should I Stay or Should I Go?: A Guide to Knowing If Your Relationship Can—and Should—Be Saved.* New York: Berkley Books, 2011.

Bancroft, Lundy. *Why Does He Do That? Inside the Minds of Angry and Controlling Men.* New York: Putnam, 2002.

Dugan, Meg Kennedy and Roger Hock. *It's My Life Now: Starting Over After an Abusive Relationship or Domestic Violence.* New York: Routledge, 2000.

Evans, Patricia. *The Verbally Abusive Relationship: How to Recognize It and How to Respond.* Avon, MA: Adams Media, 2010.

Leventhal, Beth and Sandra Lundy. *Same-Sex Domestic Violence: Strategies for Change.* Thousand Oaks, CA: Sage Publications, 1995.

NiCarthy, Ginny. *Getting Free: You Can End Abuse and Take Back Your Life.* Berkeley: Seal Press, 2004.

White, Evelyn C, *Chain, Chain, Change: For Black Women in Abusive Relationships*, Seattle: Seal Press, 1995.

Zambrano, Myrna. *Mejor Sola Que Mal Acompanada: para la mujer golpeada / For the Latina in an Abusive Relationship.* Seattle: Seal Press, 1993.

## Books on Mental Health and Trauma

Alberti, Robert and Michael Emmons. *Your Perfect Right: Assertiveness and Equality in Your Life and Relationships*. Oakland, CA: Impact, 2008.

Brenner, Helene G. *I Know I'm in There Somewhere: A Woman's Guide to Finding Her Inner Voice and Living a Life of Authenticity*. New York: Gotham, 2003.

Frederick, Ronald J. *Living Like You Mean It: Use the Wisdom and Power of Your Emotions to Get the Life You Really Want*. Hoboken, NJ: Jossey-Bass, 2009.

Herman, Judith Lewis. *Trauma and Recovery: The Aftermath of Violence from Domestic Abuse to Political Terror*. New York: Basic Books, 1992.

Kubany, Edward S., Mari A. McCaig, and Janet R. Laconsay. *Healing the Trauma of Domestic Violence: A Workbook for Women*. Oakland, CA: New Harbinger, 2004.

McKay, Mathew, Jeffrey C. Wood, and Jeffrey Brantley. *The Dialectical Behavior Therapy Skills Workbook: Practical DBT Exercises for Learning Mindfulness, Interpersonal Effectiveness, Emotion Regulation, & Distress Tolerance*. Oakland, CA: New Harbinger, 2007.

Schwartz, Richard C. *You Are the One You've Been Waiting For: Bringing Courageous Love to Intimate Relationships*. Oak Park, IL: Center for Self Leadership, 2008.

Shapiro, Francine. *Getting Past Your Past: Take Control of Your Life with Self-Help Techniques from EMDR Therapy*. Emmaus, PA: Rodale, 2012.

van der Kolk, Bessel. *The Body Keeps the Score: Brain, Mind, and Body in the Healing of Trauma*. New York: Viking, 2014.

Williams, Mary Beth and Soili Poijula. *The PTSD Workbook: Simple, Effective Techniques for Overcoming Traumatic Stress Symptoms*. Oakland, CA: New Harbinger, 2002.

## Books on Alcoholism

Fletcher, Anne M. *Sober for Good: New Solutions for Drinking Problems—Advice from Those Who Have Succeeded*. New York: Houghton Mifflin, 2001.

Knapp, Caroline. *Drinking: A Love Story*. New York: Bantam Dell, 1997.

Powter, Susan. *Sober…and Staying That Way: The Missing Link in the Cure for Alcoholism*. New York: Fireside, 1999.

Solomon, Melanie. *AA: Not the Only Way—Your One Stop Resource Guide to 12-Step Alternatives*. Fairbanks, AK: Capalo, 2008.

## Websites on Addiction

**The Addiction Recovery Guide:** www.addictionrecoveryguide.org

**Alcoholics Anonymous (AA):** http://www.aa.org

**SMART Recovery:** http://www.smartrecovery.org

## Books on Parenting

Bancroft, Lundy. *When Dad Hurts Mom: Helping Your Children Heal the Wounds of Witnessing Abuse*. New York: Berkley, 2005.

Faber, Adele and Elaine Mazlish. *How to Talk So Kids Will Listen & Listen So Kids Will Talk*, New York: Scribner, 2012.

Leman, Kevin. *Be the Dad She Needs You to Be*. Nashville: W Publishing, 2014.

Meeker, Meg, M.D. *Strong Mothers, Strong Sons: Lessons Mothers Need To Raise Extraordinary Men*. New York: Ballantine Books, 2015.

Siegel, Daniel J. and Mary Hartzell. *Parenting from the Inside Out*. New York: Penguin, 2004.

Silverstein, Olga and Beth Rashbaum. *The Courage to Raise Good Men*. New York: Penguin, 1995.

## Websites on Parenting

**Love and Logic Institute:** https://www.loveandlogic.com

**National Parent Helpline: 1-855-427-2736,** http://www.nationalparenthelpline.org

## E-mail Services for Co-Parenting After Divorce

**Our Family Wizard:** http://www.ourfamilywizard.com

**Talking Parents:** http://www.talkingparents.com

## Child Protection and Custody

Child Protection and Custody Conducted by National Council of Juvenile and Family Court Judges: 800-527-3423, http://www.ncjfcj.org

Custody Preparation for Moms: http://www.custodyprepformoms.org

Lundy Bancroft: http://www.lundybancroft.com

National Child Traumatic Stress Network: http://www.nctsn.org

National Resource Center on Domestic Violence: http://www.nrcdv.org. For culturally specific resource centers, go to http://www.nrcdv.org/dvrn and scroll down

## Mental Health and Trauma Treatment—Finding a Therapist (For Adults and Children)

Accelerated Experiential Dynamic Psychotherapy (AEDP): http://www.aedpinstitute.org/find-an-aedp-institute-therapist/

Eye Movement Desensitization and Reprocessing (EMDR): http://www.emdr.com/find-a-clinician/

Internal Family Systems: http://www.selfleadership.org/find-an-ifs-therapist.html

Psychology Today: https://therapists.psychologytoday.com/rms/

New England Society for the Treatment of Trauma and Dissociation: http://www.nesttd-online.org and select the Find a Therapist tab

Sensorimotor Psychotherapy: https://www.sensorimotorpsychotherapy.org and select the Find a SP Therapist tab

## Books on Yoga and Stress-Reduction

Emerson, David and Elizabeth Hopper. *Overcoming Trauma through Yoga: Reclaiming Your Body*. Berkeley: North Atlantic, 2011.
Stahl, Bob and Elisha Goldstein. *A Mindfulness-Based Stress Reduction Workbook*. Oakland, CA: New Harbinger, 2010.

## Website on Meditation Practice

Headspace: http://www.headspace.com

## Timelines for the Battered Women's Movement

Legislative highlights put together by New York City Department of Social Services: http://www.ncdsv.org/images/NYCHRADSS _TImelineBWM_2008.pdf.

Domestic Violence Prevention: A History of Milestones and Achievements: http://www.vawnet.org/domestic-violence /DVPreventionTimeline/

## Books for Mental Health Professionals

Dutton, Mary Ann. *Empowering and Healing the Battered Woman*. New York: Springer, 1992.

Jordan, Carol E., Michael T. Nietzel, Robert Walker, and TK Logan. *Intimate Partner Violence: A Clinical Training Guide for Mental Health Professionals*. New York: Springer, 2004.

Knudson-Martin, Carmen and Anne Rankin Mahoney, eds. *Couples, Gender, and Power: Creating Change in Intimate Relationships*. New York: Springer, 2009.

Kubany, Edward S. and Tyler C. Ralston. *Treating PTSD in Battered Women: A Step-by-Step Manual for Therapists & Counselors*. Oakland, CA: New Harbinger, 2008.

Mitchell, Connie and Deirdre Anglin, eds. *Intimate Partner Violence: A Health-Based Perspective*. New York: Oxford, 2009.

O'Leary, K. Daniel and Roland D. Maiuro, eds. *Psychological Abuse in Violent Domestic Relations*. New York: Springer, 2001.

Russell, Diana E.H. *Rape in Marriage*. Bloomington: Indiana University Press, 1990.

Taylor, Kathleen. *Brainwashing: The Science of Thought Control*. New York: Oxford, 2004.

Walker, Lenore E. A. *The Battered Woman Syndrome*. New York: Springer, 2009.

# References

APA. 2013. *DSM-5: Diagnostic and Statistical Manual of Mental Disorders, Fifth Edition.* Washington, DC: American Psychiatric Publishing.

Amnesty International. 1973. *Report on Torture.* New York: Farrar, Straus and Giroux.

Baldry, A. C. 2003. "'Sticks and Stones Hurt My Bones but His Glance and Words Hurt More': The Impact of Psychological Abuse and Physical Violence by Former and Current Partners on Battered Women in Italy." *International Journal of Forensic Mental Health* 2: 47–57.

Bancroft, Lundy. 2002. *Why Does He Do That? Inside the Minds of Angry and Controlling Men.* New York: Putnam.

Basile, K., D. Arias, S. Desai, M. Thompson. 2004. "The Differential Association of Intimate Partner Physical, Sexual, Psychological and Stalking Violence and Posttraumatic Stress Symptoms in a Nationally Representative Sample of Women." *Journal of Traumatic Stress* 17(5): 413–21.

Bergen, R. 2004. "Studying Wife Rape: Reflections on the Past, Present, and Future." *Violence Against Women* 10(12): 1407–16.

Bird, C. 1999. "Gender, Household, and Psychological Disease: The Impact of the Amount and Division of Housework." *Journal of Health and Social Behavior* 40: 32–45.

Breiding, M.J., et al. 2014. "Prevalence and Characteristics of Sexual Violence, Stalking and Intimate Partner Violence Victimization." *Morbidity and Mortality Weekly Report* 63(SS080): 1–18.

Campbell, J. C., S. W. Webster, J. Koziol-McLain, et al. 2003. "Risk Factors for Femicide Within Physically Abuse Intimate Relationships." *American Journal of Public Health* 93(7): 1089–97.

Caruso, K. 2016. "Domestic Violence and Suicide." http://www.suicide.org/domestic-violence-and-suicide.html.

CDC (Centers for Disease Control and Prevention). 2008. "Adverse Health Conditions and Health Risk Behaviors Associated with Intimate Partner Violence," *Morbidity and Mortality Weekly Report.* https://www.cdc.gov/mmwr/preview/mmwrhtml/mm5705a1.htm.

——. 2010. "The National Intimate Partner and Sexual Violence Survey." http://www.cdc.gov/violenceprevention/pdf/nisvs_report 2010-a.pdf.

——. 2016. "Definitions: Sexual Violence." http://www.cdc.gov/ViolencePrevention/sexualviolence/definitions.html.

——. 2016. "Intimate Partner Violence." http://www.cdc.gov/ViolencePrevention/intimatepartnerviolence/index.html.

Coker, A. L., P. H. Smith, L. Bethea, M. R. King, and R. E. McKeown. 2000. "Physical Health Consequences of Physical and Psychological Intimate Partner Violence." *Archive of Family Medicine.* 9(5):451–7.

Cooke, L. P. 2006. "'Doing' Gender in Context: Household Bargaining and Risk of Divorce in Germany and the United States. *American Journal of Sociology* 112: 442–72.

Coontz, S. 2005. *Marriage, a history: From Obedience to Intimacy or How Love Conquered Marriage.* New York: Viking.

Dutton, M. A. 1992. *Empowering and Healing the Battered Woman: A Model for Assessment and Intervention.* New York: Springer.

Frisco, M. and K. Williams. 2003. "Perceived Household Equity, Marital Happiness, and Divorce in Dual-Earner Households." *Journal of Family Issues* 24: 51–73.

Gazmararian J. A. I., et al. 2000. "Violence and Reproductive Health." *Journal of Maternal Child Health.* 4(2): 79–84.

Gergen, K. 1999. *An Invitation to Social Construction.* Newbury Park, CA: Sage.

Greenberg, L. S. and R. N. Goldman. 2008. *Emotion-Focused Couples Therapy: The Dynamics of Emotion, Love, and Power.* Washington, DC: American Psychological Association.

Gottman, J. M. and N. Silver. 1999. *The Seven Principles for Making Marriage Work.* New York: Harmony.

Gulley, N. 2011. "New York Law Now Makes Choking a Crime, Results in 2000 Arrests." http://www.reuters.com/article/us-strangulation-newyork-idUSTRE7367H020110407.

Haddock, S. A., and S. W. Bowling. 2001. "Therapists' Approaches to the Normative Challenges of Dual-Earner Couples: Negotiating

Outdated Societal Ideologies." *Balancing Family and Work: Special Considerations in Feminist Therapy.* New York: Haworth Press.

Herman, J. 1992. *Trauma and Recovery: The Aftermath of Violence from Domestic Abuse to Political Terror.* New York: Basic Books.

Jordan, J. V., A. G. Kaplan, J. B. Miller, I. P. Stiver, and J. L. Surrey. 1991. *Women's Growth In Connection: Writings from the Stone Center.* New York: Guilford Press.

Katz, J., I. Arias, and S. Beach. 2000. "Psychological Abuse, Self-Esteem, and Women's Dating Relationship Outcomes: A Comparison of the Self-Verification and Self-Enhancement Perspectives." *Psychology of Women Quarterly* 24: 349–57.

Kiecolt-Glaser, J. and T. Newton. 2001. "Marriage and health: His and Hers." *Psychological Bulletin* 127: 472–503.

Logan, T., J. Cole, and A. Capillo. 2007. "A Differential Characteristics of Intimate Partner, Acquaintance and Stranger Rape Survivors Examined By a Sexual Assault Nurse Examiner (SANE)." *Journal of Interpersonal Violence* 22: 1066–76.

Lynch, S. 1998. "Who Supports Whom? How Age and Gender Affect the Perceived Quality of Support of Family and Friends." *The Gerontologist* 38: 231–38.

Marshall, L. L. 1999. Effects of Men's Subtle and Overt Psychological Abuse on Low-Income Women. *Violence Victimization* 14(1): 69–88.

———. 1996. "Psychological Abuse and Women: Six Distinct Clusters." *Journal of Family Violence* 11: 4.

McFarlane, J. and A. Malecha. 2005. *Sexual Assault Among Intimates: Frequency, Consequences and Treatments,* unpublished report made available by the National Criminal Justice Reference Service.

McKibbin, C. 1998. "The Relationship of Subtle and Overt Psychological Abuse to Women's Self-Concept and Psychological Symptoms." *Dissertation Abstracts International; Section B: The Sciences and Engineering,* 58(7-B): 3968.

*Merriam-Webster Dictionary, The.* 2016. Merriam-Webster, Inc: Springfield, MA.

New York City Department of Social Services. 2008. "Timeline of the Battered Women's Movement." http://www.ncdsv.org/images /NYCHRADSS_TImelineBWM_2008.pdf.

NiCarthy, G., K. Merriam, and S. Coffman. 1984. *Talking It Out: A Guide to Groups for Abused Women.* Berkeley: Seal Press.

Ovara, T. A., P. J. McLeod, and D. Sharpe. 1996. "Perception of Control, Depressive Symptomatology and Self-Esteem of Women in Transition from Abusive Relationships." *Journal of Family Violence* 11: 167–86.

Hamby, S., D. Finkelhor, H. Turner, and D. Ormrod. 2011. "Children's Exposure to Intimate Partner Violence and Other Family Violence." https://www.ncjrs.gov/pdffiles1/ojjdp/232272.pdf.

Pico-Alfonso, M. 2005. "Psychological Intimate Partner Violence: The Major Predictor of Posttraumatic Stress Disorder in Abused Women." *Neuroscience and Biobehavioral Reviews* 29(1): 181–93.

Plichta, S. B. 2004. "Intimate Partner Violence and Physical Health Consequences: Policy and Practice Implications." *Journal of Interpersonal Violence* 19(11): 1296–323.

Postmus J. L., et al. 2012. "Understand Economic Abuse in the Lives of Survivors." *Journal of Interpersonal Violence*. 27(3): 411–30.

Russell, D. 1990. *Rape in Marriage*. Bloomington: Indiana University Press.

Sackett, L. A., and D. G. Saunders. 2001. "The Impact of Different Forms of Psychological Abuse on Battered Women." *Psychological Abuse in Violent Domestic Relationships*. New York: Springer.

Shapiro, F. 2001. *Eye Movement Desensitization and Reprocessing: Basic Principles, Protocols, and Procedures*. New York: Guilford Press.

Steil, J. 1997. *Marital Equality: Its Relationship to the Well-Being of Husbands and Wives*. Newbury Park, CA: SAGE Publications.

Taylor, K. 2004. *Brainwashing: The Science of Thought Control*. New York: Oxford.

United States Department of Justice. 2015. "Domestic Violence." https://www.justice.gov/ovw/domestic-violence.

van der Kolk, Bessel. 2014. *The Body Keeps the Score: Brain, Mind, and Body in the Healing of Trauma*. New York: Viking.

Walker, Lenore E. 1980. *The Battered Woman*. New York: William Morrow.

White House, The. 2016. "Factsheet: The Violence Against Women Act." https://www.whitehouse.gov/sites/default/files/docs/vawa_factsheet.pdf.

WomenSafe. 2016. "Overview of Historical Laws that Supported Domestic Violence." http://www.womensafe.net/home/index.php/domesticviolence/29-overview-of-historical-laws-that-supported-domestic-violence.

**Carol A. Lambert, MSW,** is a psychotherapist and domestic violence expert with three decades of clinical experience helping individuals and groups, and a career-long commitment to women's psychological health. Since 1993, she developed a unique approach and cofounded the Recovery Groups for Women with Controlling Partners that bring together insights from mental health, trauma recovery, and domestic violence. At McLean Hospital, a psychiatric hospital affiliated with Harvard Medical School, she provides domestic violence training and consultation. Over the years, her expertise took her from educating volunteers in a domestic violence program affiliated with local police to providing training and consultation to the National Football League. In all her endeavors, she brings critical attention to psychological abuse and the major losses to women's mental and physical health. She's currently in private clinical practice in Belmont and Concord, MA.

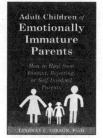

Register your **new harbinger** titles for additional benefits!

When you register your **new harbinger** title—purchased in any format, from any source—you get access to benefits like the following:

- Downloadable accessories like printable worksheets and extra content
- Instructional videos and audio files
- Information about updates, corrections, and new editions

Not every title has accessories, but we're adding new material all the time.

Access free accessories in 3 easy steps:

1. Sign in at NewHarbinger.com (or **register** to create an account).

2. Click on **register a book**. Search for your title and click the **register** button when it appears.

3. Click on the **book cover or title** to go to its details page. Click on **accessories** to view and access files.

That's all there is to it!

If you need help, visit:

NewHarbinger.com/accessories

**new harbinger**
CELEBRATING
**40** YEARS